BEAUTY FOR ASHES

Beauty for Ashes

The Christ-life for the self-life

ZAC POONEN

KINGSWAY PUBLICATIONS
EASTBOURNE

Published in India by Gospel Literature Service

First British edition 1980

ISBN 0 86065 104 5

Printed in Great Britain for
KINGSWAY PUBLICATIONS LTD
Lottbridge Drove, Eastbourne, E. Sussex BN23 6NT by
Richard Clay (The Chaucer Press) Ltd, Bungay, Suffolk

To ANNIE

my devoted helpmeet,
who has faithfully stood behind the scenes
and upheld me in my ministry.

The mouth could not speak,
neither could the hand write,
if the heart did not pump the life-blood to them.

Contents

The Lord hath anointed me [*Jesus*] . . .
to give unto them beauty for ashes.
(Isaiah 61:1, 3.)

Introduction

God had a great and glorious purpose for man when he created him. Of all created beings, as far as we know, man alone was created with the capacity to share in God's life and partake of the divine nature. But he could enjoy this privilege only as he voluntarily chose to live a life centred on God.

The two trees in the garden of Eden were symbolic of two principles of life. Adam could either partake of the tree of life (which symbolized God himself) and live by the divine life, or else he could choose the tree of knowledge of good and evil, and thus develop his own self-life and live independently of God. As we all know, he chose the latter. Being descended from Adam, we all have this over-developed self-life now.

But God's purpose for man did not change when Adam fell. The coming of Christ into the world was in order that we might be delivered from this self-centred life that we have inherited, and once again have the opportunity to partake of the tree of life. This is the abundant life that Christ offers us.

Isaiah had prophesied (61:1-3) that Christ, when he came, would set people free from bondage. Man is bound not only by the devil but also by his self-life. Christ has come to set us free from both. Isaiah said that Christ would give those he liberated *beauty* to replace their *ashes*. Ashes are a most appropriate symbol of the self-life—picturing its ugliness and its uselessness. Christ offers to give us the beauty of his own life to replace the ashes. What a privilege! Yet many Christians do not enjoy this fully. Why not? How can we enjoy it?

That is the subject of this book.

We shall look at four characters from the Bible in the pages that follow: and each of them will have something to teach us.

1. The corruption of the self-life

We can never enjoy deliverance from our self-life before we see something of its total corruption. Let us look at the elder son in the parable in Luke 15, for he illustrates perhaps better than anyone else in the Bible the utter rottenness of the self-life.

The younger son in the parable is usually considered the worse of the two boys. But as we look a little more carefully at the elder brother, we discover that he was just as bad—if not worse. True, he did not commit the same sins as his younger brother. But his heart was just as crooked and self-centred.

Man's total depravity

The human heart is basically the same in every individual. When the Bible describes the human heart as deceitful above all things and desperately wicked (Jer 17:9), it refers to every child of Adam. The refinements of civilization, lack of opportunity to commit sin and a sheltered upbringing may perhaps have kept some from falling into the grosser sins that others have fallen into. But we cannot, on that count, consider ourselves better than others. For if we had had the same upbringing as theirs, and if we had faced the same pressures, we would have probably ended up committing the same sins. This may be a humiliating fact to acknowledge, but is nevertheless true.

The sooner we recognize this fact, the sooner we shall experience deliverance. Paul recognized that no good thing dwelt in his flesh (Rom 7:18). That was his first step to freedom (Rom 8:2).

Men look on the outward appearance and call some good and others bad. But God who looks at the heart sees all men in the same condition. The Bible teaches the total depravity of all men. Consider Romans 3:10-12, for example: 'There is none righteous,' (and just in case we think that is an overstatement, he goes on to say), '*no, not one.* There is *none* that understandeth, there is *none* that seeketh after God' (AV). 'All have turned aside, together they have gone wrong; no one does good, *not even one.*' Romans 3:10-20 is a summing-up of the guilt of all humanity—of the irreligious as well as the religious. In Romans 1:18-32 we have a description of 'the younger son'—the externally immoral and godless man. In chapter 2, we have a portrayal of 'the elder son'—the religious man who nevertheless is equally a sinner. After having described these two categories of people, the Holy Spirit sums up the case by saying that both groups are alike guilty. There is no difference between one and the other.

Man is indeed totally depraved; and if God does not reach down and do something for him, there is certainly no hope for him.

Self-centredness

The elder son (Lk 15:25-32) can be taken to symbolize an active Christian. If the father in the story is a type of God, it would be legitimate to consider the son as a type of a child of God—a Christian. And an active Christian at that—for we see him in the parable coming home after a day's work in his father's fields. Here was no lazy young man, sitting at home and enjoying his father's wealth. Here was one who worked hard for his father, one who *apparently* loved his father more than his younger brother did—for after all, he did not leave home and waste his father's wealth. Apparently more devoted, but actually, as we shall see, just as selfish as his younger brother. It is the picture of a believer active in the Lord's work and apparently full of devotion to his Lord but still centred in himself.

God has created this world with certain laws built into it. If we ignore those laws, we shall undoubtedly suffer some form of loss and injury. For example, God has ordained that the earth should revolve around the sun. If the earth had a will of its own and decided one day that it would no longer be centred on the sun, but would merely revolve around itself, there would then be no change of seasons and very soon all life on earth would perish. Death would enter in.

Adam, likewise, was created to be centred on God. The day he refused that Centre and chose to be centred on himself—this was what was implied in his choosing to eat the fruit of the tree that God had forbidden—he died, as God had said he would.

And let us remember that there is a lesson here for us. In the measure in which our Christian life and service are centred on ourselves, in that measure we shall experience spiritual death—in spite of our being born again and in spite of our fundamentalism. And unconsciously we shall be ministering spiritual death to others too. We may have a reputation as keen and zealous workers for the Father (as the elder son perhaps had), but may nevertheless merit the rebuke of the Lord, 'I know your reputation as live and active . . . but you are dead' (Rev 3:1, TLB). This is a tragic thing, and yet dangerously possible in Christian work. Many a Christian leader lives on the reputation he has built up for himself. Looked up to by others, he is often unconscious of the fact that God sees him in an altogether different light. Never having been delivered from self-centredness himself, he is unable to deliver others—even though he may preach, or sing, beautifully. And so, for all of us, a warning is given in the story of the elder son.

Recognizing the evil within

God often allows times of pressure to come into our lives to bring up from within us our corrupt self-life, so that we begin to see ourselves as we really are. It is fairly easy for us to consider ourselves spiritual when our circumstances are easy. When we have no problems to tackle, when nobody is irritating us, when things are going smoothly and our friends are congenial, we can deceive ourselves about the real state of our hearts. But wait till we get a neighbour or a fellow-worker who annoys us all the time, and the veneer of spirituality disappears. Our self-life will then manifest itself in all its ugliness.

This was what happened to the elder son. When his younger brother was honoured, he got upset. No one would ever have thought that this elder son could have behaved so peevishly. He had appeared such a nice person all along. But he hadn't faced pressure like this before. Now his real nature was manifested. It was not the provocation at that moment that made him evil. No. The provocation merely brought to the surface what was within all the time.

Amy Carmichael once said that a cup of sweet water could never spill a drop of *bitter* water, no matter how heavily it was jolted. This is so true. If the bitter water comes out of our lives and our lips, it is because it has always been there. It is not the provocation or the irritation that makes us unspiritual. They only bring out what is within. And so it should be a matter for deep thankfulness to God that he allows such times to come upon our lives when we see the corruption of our flesh. If it were not for such occasions, we might never realize that there is a fountain of corruption in our flesh.

This also teaches us that suppression is *not* victory. One person may explode in anger in a trying situation, while another (with a little more self-control) in a similar situation may only boil inwardly, without any steam escaping through his lips! In men's eyes, the second person may have a reputation for meekness. But God who sees the hearts knows that both men boiled within. The difference in their external conduct was merely a result of different temperaments which matter nothing to God.

If suppression were victory, then I think shopkeepers, salesmen and air-hostesses are among the most Christ-like people that I have ever met! No matter how much their customers tax their patience, they still retain a gracious attitude towards them, for the sake of their business—even though they may be boiling within! No. Suppression is not victory. God does not want us merely to *appear* delivered and spiritual—but to be *actually* so. Paul said, 'It is no longer I who live, but Christ who lives in me' (Gal 2:20). This is the point to which God would bring us.

Let us look at the characteristics of the self-life in two aspects. First, its attitude towards God, and secondly, its attitude towards its fellow men. We see both of these illustrated in the story of the elder son.

THE SELF-CENTRED LIFE'S ATTITUDE TO GOD

Legalism

The attitude of the self-centred life to God and to his service is characterized by a spirit of legalism. Self can try to serve God. It can be very active in such service too—but it is always legalistic service. It seeks a reward for the service it offers to God. 'I have served you all these years,' the elder son tells the father, 'but you never gave me a kid.' He had served his father for reward all along, but it had not been evident until now. This moment of pressure brought out the fact.

That is how self serves God—not freely, joyfully and spontaneously, but hoping for a return. The return expected may even be some spiritual blessing and reward from God. But service done with even such a motive is legalistic and unacceptable to God.

The elder son considered his father hard and cruel for not having rewarded his service during all those years. He was like the man who was given one talent, who came up to his master at reckoning time and said he'd kept his talent safe without trading it for profit, 'because I was afraid you would demand my profits, for you are *a hard man to deal with*' (Lk 19:21, TLB). Self considers God to be so demanding and so difficult to please, and so it strives and strives in God's service and still condemns itself for not having satisfied the demands of such an austere God.

That is not the type of service that God expects from any of us. The Bible says, 'God loves a cheerful giver' (2 Cor 9:7). In the matter of service too God delights in one who serves cheerfully, neither grudgingly nor of necessity. He would rather have no service at all than *reluctant* service. When one serves for reward, it is but a short while before he is complaining to God that he is not being blessed sufficiently. The matter becomes worse when someone else is more blessed than he is.

Do we ever compare our work and the blessing we receive with that of others? This can only be the result of legalistic service. Jesus once told a parable about some labourers who were employed at different hours of the day by a certain man. At the end of the day the master gave them each a penny. Those who had worked longest came up to the master and complained, 'How can you give us the same wages as these other people? We deserve more.' They served for wages, and when they got what they had agreed for, they complained that others should not be given as much (Mt 20:1-16).

This is exactly what we see in the elder son: 'How can you give all this to my younger brother. I am the one who has served you faithfully, not he.'

When the Israelites served God grudgingly, he sent them into captivity as he had told them he would: 'Because you did not serve the Lord your God with joyfulness and gladness of heart . . . therefore you shall serve your enemies' (Deut 28:47-48). No. God has no pleasure in legalistic service.

Self-centred Christians often serve God in order to keep up an impression of spirituality in the eyes of others. It is not pure and fervent love for Christ that keeps them active in Christian work, but the fear that others will consider them unspiritual if they do nothing. And when such people choose an easy path for themselves and one that will bring them financial gain, they try so hard to convince everybody that God has led them that way! Why the need for such self-justification, unless there be the secret fear that others may now think less of their spirituality! What strain and bondage there is in serving God like that.

What joy and what liberty there is in service that springs out of love for Christ! Love is the oil that lubricates the machinery of our lives so that it doesn't creak or groan! Jacob laboured for seven years in order to obtain Rachel. And the Bible says that those seven years seemed to him just as a few days, because of his love for her (Gen 29:20). So will it be with us when our service for

God springs out of love. There will be no strain and no drudgery.

The Bible teaches that Christ's relationship with his church is like that of a husband and wife. What does a husband expect primarily from his wife? Not her service. He does not marry her for her to cook his food and wash his clothes, as of first importance. What he desires primarily is her love. Without that, all else is valueless. This is what God seeks from us too.

Unteachability

Another characteristic of the self-centred life is its unteachability. When the elder son was angry and stood outside the house, his father came out and entreated him. But he was stubborn and refused to listen.

Truly, 'it is better to be a poor but wise youth than to be an old and foolish king who refuses all advice' (Eccles 4:13, TLB). The one who feels that he knows everything and is therefore unwilling to learn from others is indeed in a sorry state.

The self-centred individual is so sure that he is right that he is unwilling to accept correction. And so he does not like being criticized. Our spirituality is perhaps never so tested as when we are opposed and contradicted. A. W. Tozer has said that when we are criticized, the only thing that should concern us is whether the criticism is true or false, not whether the person doing the criticizing is a friend or an enemy. Our enemies often tell us more truths about ourselves than our friends do.

An unyielding, headstrong disposition is a sure mark of the self-centred individual. And let us remember that a rigid, self-defensive attitude towards our fellow men is indicative of a similar attitude in our hearts towards God. If we are unwilling to be taught and corrected by our brethren, it only shows how wrapped-up in ourselves we are, in spite of all our spiritual experiences and Bible-knowledge.

The father pleads with the elder son, but the latter is hurt and filled with self-pity. The self-centred Christian loves to be coaxed and humoured and petted like a little child—even by God. God has to keep on pleading with such persons, but they do not listen easily. Ultimately, they may find themselves, like the elder son, outside the Father's house altogether.

Do you see how horrible the heart of man is!

THE SELF-CENTRED LIFE'S ATTITUDE TO FELLOW MEN

Jealousy and love of honour

When our fellowship with God is strained or broken, it invariably affects our relationships with our fellow men. When Adam was cut off from the life of God, he immediately lost his love for Eve too. When God asked him whether he had sinned, he accused his wife and said, 'Lord, the fault is not mine. It is this woman's.'

Jealousy is one of the characteristics of the self-centred life in its attitude to others. The elder son (in the parable) was jealous of his younger brother and this was what made him angry. All these years the elder son had been the undisputed heir in the house. The servants had bowed to him. But now his position was threatened. Someone else was now the centre of attraction in the house. And he couldn't bear to see this. Jealousy, that green-eyed monster, was quick to rear its ugly head in his heart.

The self-centred life loves to be noticed by others. It loves the praise of men, and is evidently delighted when it is the sole object of admiration. It loves the highest place and draws attention to itself perpetually in one way or another. The self-centred Christian looks for opportunities to tell others of what he has done for the Lord—perhaps in a very pious way but secretly expecting their appreciation. And he is very uneasy when someone else succeeds or has done something better than himself.

The self-centred person is easily upset and touchy. He longs to be recognized by others and to be consulted for his opinions. In fact he would be quite offended if he were not consulted in a committee meeting, for example. He has such a high opinion of himself that he loves to talk and talk, thinking that everyone else needs his valuable advice! There are Christians who, once they open their mouths, find it difficult to shut them again; and who keep on talking not realizing that everyone else around is uninterested. An uncontrolled tongue is one of the marks of an uncrucified self-life.

The self-centred Christian does not know how to take the second place graciously and joyfully. He is upset when someone else is given the leadership and he himself has to play second fiddle. The only time that he is willing to take the second place is when he knows that thereby he can step into the first place on the retirement of the leader!

It was said of the German Kaiser that he always wished to be the centre of attraction in every place. If he went to a christening, he'd wish he were the baby; if he went to a marriage, he'd wish he were the bride; and if he went to a funeral, he'd wish he were the corpse! Let us not forget that his flesh was no worse than ours.

Self-centredness in a man makes him draw the attention of others to himself, even in the most sacred of activities—whether it be preaching a sermon or writing a prayer-letter. It is this, when found in a Christian leader, that hinders the spiritual growth of those to whom he ministers—for he draws people not to Christ but to himself.

One who sat for many years under the ministry of Watchman Nee, the Chinese apostle, said that the thing that impressed him most about Nee's ministry was that he drew people beyond himself to Christ. This is what God calls each of us to do. But how few actually do this.

Hindering younger workers

A self-centred Christian leader hinders others below him from becoming leaders, in case his own position is threatened. And so he ministers in such a way as to make himself a necessity to those to whom he ministers. This is utterly contrary to God's will. Oswald Chambers once said that anyone who made himself a necessity to some other soul had got out of God's order. God alone is the only absolute necessity to any human soul. May none of us ever try to take that place.

No one is indispensable in Christ's church. God's work can easily carry on without us. In fact, it can carry on much better without the help of those conceited folk who consider themselves indispensable! We must recognize this fact constantly. And so we must be willing to withdraw into the background any time God calls us to. But the self-centred Christian worker will never accept that. He will want to hold on to his position for as long as possible. Many such 'Christian leaders' are rotting away on their 'thrones' today, hindering the work of God. They do not know what it is to fade graciously into the background and let someone else take their place.

You've probably heard the saying that success without a successor is a failure. Jesus recognized this and trained people to carry on his work. In three-and-a-half years he had trained people to take over the leadership. Paul recognized the necessity of training other people to carry on the work. In 2 Timothy 2:2 he says, 'Now Timothy, what I have committed to you, I want you to pass on to other people who will in turn be able to train others (right on up to the fourth generation)' (paraphrase). What Paul was saying in effect was, 'You must ensure that you commit this treasure to others. Don't ever hinder people younger than you from coming up.' Even people in the business world recognize this principle. But many Christian leaders do not. Truly 'the children of this world are in their generation wiser than the children of light'.

It is indeed nothing but self-centredness that makes a man jealous of someone younger doing things better than he. Cain was jealous of the fact that Abel had been accepted by God and that he himself had been rejected. If Abel had been older, that might have been tolerable. But it was the awful fact that his *younger* brother was better that made him furious enough to slay Abel.

We see the same in the case of Joseph and his brothers. Joseph received divine revelations, and that made all his ten elder brothers green with jealousy and they tried to do away with him.

King Saul was jealous of young David, because the women sang, 'Saul has slain thousands while David has slain *ten* thousands.' From that day he determined to kill him. Man's history—and alas, the history of the Christian church too—is filled with the same story over and over again.

On the other hand, what a refreshing contrast it is to look at a man like Barnabas in the New Testament. He was a senior worker who took the newly converted Paul of Tarsus under his wing when no one else would accept him. Barnabas brought him to the church in Antioch and encouraged him. In Acts 13 we read that Barnabas and Paul went out together on a missionary journey. And when Barnabas saw that God was calling this junior worker, Paul, to a larger ministry than his own, he willingly stepped back and graciously faded into the background. And the phrase 'Barnabas and Paul' changes almost unnoticed to 'Paul and Barnabas' in the book of Acts. The Christian church suffers today because there are few like Barnabas who know what it is to step back and let another be honoured. We are willing to step back in matters of no importance. When passing through a door, for example, we don't mind stepping back and permitting another to go through first. But in the realms that matter—such as position and leadership in the church—we are not so ready to step back. Our self-life is so deceitful. We can have a false humility in things that don't count for much.But it is in important matters that we see ourselves as we really are.

Pride

The self-centred person has an exalted opinion of himself. The elder son said, 'All these years I've worked hard for you and never once refused to do a single thing you told me to.' He was proud of his obedient service to his father. Pride arises in our hearts, not because of our virtues and our successes alone, but also because we feel that others around us have not done as well as we have. Pride is always the result of a comparison of ourselves with others. If others around us were obviously better than us, we would never feel proud. If there had been another brother in this story who had served the father more faithfully than the elder son, the latter could not have felt proud at all in the presence of the other. But here, he felt, he could compare himself favourably with his younger brother. 'I have served you faithfully,' he tells his father, 'but look at this younger son of yours. What has he done? He has wasted his money on harlots.'

It was through pride that Lucifer fell. He compared himself with the other angels and felt that he was wiser, more beautiful and more exalted than them all. He was the anointed cherub, but he became the devil. Many others since have lost God's anointing in the same manner. You may be like an angel, but pride can turn you into a devil.

This was the disease that the Pharisees were plagued with. Jesus portrayed them accurately in the parable where the Pharisee prays, 'Lord, I thank thee that I am not like other men. I fast and pray and tithe etc.,' . . . ad nauseam. The self-life is like that. Sometimes, however, it can be more subtle—as in the case of the Sunday-school teacher who after teaching this parable to her class prayed, 'Lord, we thank thee that we are not like the Pharisees.' We can laugh at that because we say inwardly, 'Thank God I'm not like that Sunday-school teacher'!

Pride often manifests itself in such humble garb. The self-centred Christian worker is not necessarily one who goes about with an overbearing attitude. He has plenty of false humility on the exterior, a pious lowly appearance and 'humble' talk. But inwardly, he compares himself with others and glories in his goodness and greatness and 'humility'!

Condemnation of others

Such comparison of ourselves with others finally leads to condemnation of others—sometimes with harsh bitterness. Listen to what the elder son tells his father: 'This younger son of yours has wasted your money on harlots.' Who had given him that information? No one. He had merely assumed the worst. When you hate someone, it is easy to believe the worst possible things concerning him. How the elder son delighted to expose his younger brother's faults, instead of covering them.

Do we see only the faults in other people? Have we secretly delighted in seeing another fall—particularly if he was one whom we did not like? Our flesh is so corrupt that when other people fall, it does not grieve us entirely—on the contrary we may be slightly pleased, for it shows us up as better men. Such an attitude is characteristic of a self-centred person.

Do we judge the motives of others? The self-centred person sees someone doing something and says to himself, 'I know *why* he's doing that,' and proceeds to impute some carnal motive to the action. How much the self-life takes upon itself—even to sit upon the throne of God (for after all, it is God alone who can judge the motives of others). Paul warns us, 'Be careful not to jump to conclusions before the Lord returns as to whether someone is a good servant or not. When the Lord comes, he will turn on the light so that everyone can see exactly what each one of us is really like, deep down in our hearts. Then everyone will know why we have been doing the Lord's work' (1 Cor 4:5, TLB). Only when the Lord returns (and not till then) will we know the real motives of each person.

Lovelessness

The self-centred person does not have any *real* love for his fellow men, and this is the root cause of his hard attitude towards them. He may pretend to show much love, but lacks genuine Christ-like love. The elder son had never gone to his father even once in all those years, volunteering to go and search for his lost brother. He did not care whether his brother was dead or alive. All he was interested in was to make merry with his friends (Lk 15:29). So long as he himself was happy, it did not matter to him what happened to others.

Are we wrapped up in ourselves like that? What is our attitude to backsliders? It is easier to love an unbeliever than a backslider. But if we truly have the compassion of Christ, we shall love both. The younger son in this story is a picture of a backslider. It's easy to condemn him. It is more difficult to love him and help him. The Bible says, 'If a Christian is overcome by some sin, you who are godly should gently and humbly help him back on to the right path' (Gal 6:1, TLB). And again, 'If you see a Christian sinning . . . you should ask God to forgive him and God will give him life' (1 Jn 5:16, TLB). Do we ever pray like that for those who have fallen? No? Why not? Because we are so centred in ourselves.

When we seek for a deeper life and a closer walk with God, let us never forget that a deeper life should make us more outgoing. God does not grant us a closer walk with him merely for us to 'make merry with our friends'. It is so easy for us to get into our little holy huddles (with those who believe as we do) and to think of our enjoyment alone—all the time looking down on those who have not had our 'deeper-life experience'. That is not the deeper life at all. That is self-centredness under the guise of spirituality; and it is an abomination to God.

Let us not be deceived. If we are only interested in 'making merry' (even when it is spiritual merry-making) with other members of our spiritual clique, and are unable to fellowship with believers who do not see eye-to-eye with us, then we are indeed in a state of spiritual stagnation. The Bible says, 'He who does not love [his brother] remains in death' (1 Jn 3:14). The word translated 'love' in this verse is a Greek word which means 'to value', 'to feel a concern for', 'to be faithful to' and 'to delight in'. And so this verse really means that if we do not value our brothers and sisters, or feel a concern for them, if we are not faithful to them and fail to delight in them, then, in spite of all our Bible-knowledge and our spiritual experiences, we are in a state of spiritual death.

The primary ministry of the Holy Spirit

We may be young or old, with any number of experiences

and blessings to our credit, but self dies hard, I'll tell you that. We must know what it is to take up the cross daily and follow Jesus if we are to live in victory over self. There is no other way. We shall come to that in greater detail in later chapters.

But let us remember this meanwhile, that the primary ministry of the Holy Spirit in our lives is to help us overcome our self-centredness. The Bible says, 'We naturally love to do evil things that are just the opposite of the things that the Holy Spirit tells us to do; and the good things we want to do when the Spirit has his way with us are just the opposite of our natural desires. These two forces within [our self-life and the Holy Spirit] are constantly fighting each other to win control over us' (Gal 5:17, TLB). In these days particularly, when many Christians are confused about the ministry of the Holy Spirit, it is good for us to bear in mind that his chief ministry is to help us put to death the deeds of the body (the self-life). He does many other things in and through us. Let us not despise any of them. But this is his primary ministry—to put the self-life to death—and if we are not allowing him to carry out this in our lives, then all our other experiences are worthless.

The Bible says, 'If you live according to the flesh you will die, but if by the Spirit you put to death the deeds of the body you will live. For all who are led by the Spirit of God [in this way] are the sons of God' (Rom 8:13-14). Verse 14 is often quoted out of context and made to refer to the Spirit's guidance in relation to where we are to go or what we are to do. But it is really connected with the previous verse and refers to the Holy Spirit leading us to put to death our self-centred desires. The verse also teaches that *this* is the identifying mark of the sons of God.

In the parable in Luke 15, we notice that the father's love was the same for both his sons. He did not love the elder son any less than the younger. He came out of his house for both his children. When his younger son came home, he went out of the house to welcome him, and when his elder son refused to come into the house, he went out to invite him in too. In fact he even tells him, 'Son, you are ever with me and all that I have is yours.' Do you see the largeness of God's heart even towards self-centred individuals? He loves us and wants to give us all he has. But he has to deliver us from our self-centredness first.

God does not love the harlot more than the self-righteous Pharisee. He loves both equally and he gave his Son to die for both. But the response in the hearts of the two may be different; and that is what makes the difference ultimately in the Father's house. The younger son who was once away from the father's house is now sitting at the table enjoying his father's riches. The elder son who had been inside all along is now outside. Truly, as the Lord said, many who are first now will be last in eternity, and many who are last here will be first there. It is only as we are willing to humble ourselves and acknowledge our corruption and respond wholeheartedly to the Father's love, that we shall be able to feast with him at his table.

May the Lord speak to our hearts.

2. The pathway to the Christ-life (a) Being broken

One of the verses which clearly describes the pathway that leads us out of the corruption of our self-life into the full beauty of the Christ-life is Galatians 2:20—'I am crucified with Christ: nevertheless I live. Yet not I, but Christ liveth in me' (AV). To us, this may be merely a good verse to be memorized or to get three points for a sermon from! But to the apostle Paul who wrote it, it described his experience. He had exchanged the ashes of his self-life for the beauty of Christ's own divine life. And this had become possible for him because he had accepted death to himself.

It is only when the 'I' (the self-life) is crucified that Christ can manifest himself in his glory within us. In 2 Corinthians 3:18 we read that the Holy Spirit transforms us into the image of Christ from one degree of glory to another. Day by day, and year by year, the Spirit of God seeks to conform us increasingly to the likeness of Christ. But the pathway from each step of glory to the next is via the cross. If we through the Spirit put to death our self-life, we shall know the abundance of Christ's life; not otherwise.

We can no longer go freely to the tree of life as Adam could, before he fell. In Genesis 3:24 we read that God placed a flaming sword in front of the tree of life. And so, before we can partake of this tree, the flaming sword has to fall upon and slay our self-life. There is no other way to reach the life of God. The way of the cross is the only way to fullness of life. This truth is taught in plain words as well as in symbol, throughout the Scriptures, from Genesis to Revelation. The cross *breaks us* as well as *empties us.* We shall consider these two aspects of the cross in this chapter and the next.

Jacob's two meetings with God

Jacob was a man who learnt experimentally what it means to be broken. We can learn many truths from his life.

One excellent thing about the Bible is that it is absolutely honest in recording the faults and failings of its greatest men. The Scriptures do not portray marble saints. We see in the word of God men and women exactly as they were—warts and all. This is why the biographies of biblical characters are a greater encouragement to us than many biographies written in our day (which tend to hide the failings of the men they describe, and present them as super-saints).

Jacob was a man of like passions as we are. He was called by God, no doubt, and eternally predestined to be a chosen vessel for the working out of the divine purposes. But he had a corrupt and deceitful heart, like all men. God calls ordinary people to his service—not supermen. Very often, he calls the base and the despised and the weak of the world, to fulfil his purposes. He puts no premium whatever on human cleverness and ability in his service.

Jacob must have met with God many times in his life. But in the record given us in Genesis, there are two meetings with God that stand out. The first at Bethel, where he dreamt of a ladder reaching up to heaven, and where he said, 'This is the house of God' (Gen 28:10-22).

The second at Peniel, where he wrestled with God and where he said, 'I have seen God face to face' (Gen 32:22-32). Between these two incidents lay twenty years.

At Bethel, we read, he stopped to camp, when the *sun had set* (Gen 28:11). That of course is only a statement indicating the time of day at which Jacob arrived at Bethel. But as we read the subsequent record of Jacob's life (in the next four chapters) we find that the sun had indeed set upon his life. And during the twenty years that followed this incident, the darkness grew deeper and deeper. But that was not the end of the story.

At Peniel he met with God again. And there, it is recorded, immediately after his meeting with God, *the sun rose*, and he journeyed on (Gen 32:31). Again a geographical fact—but true of Jacob's life as well. He was a different man from that day. The darkness passed away and the light of God shone upon his life.

God has given us the record of Jacob's darkness to show us that he was an ordinary man. He experienced the same darkness that we do. But he experienced a sunrise as well. And this encourages us to believe that no matter how great the darkness of our self-life, we can yet see the rising of the sun, if we will follow in Jacob's footsteps at Peniel. Let us then look at Jacob's life—first when the sun had set on him; and secondly when the sun rose.

THE SUN SETS

Jacob came out of his mother's womb, grabbing his brother's leg. 'So they called him Jacob (meaning "Grabber")' (Gen 25:26, TLB). And that is exactly what he was. He was always grabbing something from someone for himself. He grabbed the birthright from his brother and later the blessing from his father. He grabbed Rachel from her father Laban, and later grabbed

Laban's property as well.

Jacob was a *bargainer* too. He bargained with Esau for the birthright. And later, he bargained with Laban for Rachel. At Bethel, we find him even bargaining with God.

Jacob was also a *deceiver*. When he wanted his father's blessing, he was prepared to deceive his father in order to get it. He was even prepared to take the name of God in telling the lie. When Isaac asks him how he got the meat so quickly, he replies, 'The Lord thy God brought it to me' (Gen 27:20, AV). How lightly he could even swear and tell a lie! He certainly had no fear of God.

Such was Jacob's nature—grabbing, bargaining and deceiving—looking after his own earthly interests all the time. He was very much a child of Adam.

Coming short of God's calling

Finally, at Bethel, the sun set upon his life. There, in a dream, God gave Jacob a revelation of his great and glorious purpose for his life. He gave Jacob the same promises that he had given Abraham. But how does Jacob respond? He says, in effect, 'Lord, I'm not so interested in all those spiritual blessings. If you'll only protect me from harm and danger and give me food to eat and clothes to wear, I'll be quite happy. I'll give you one-tenth of my income and acknowledge you as my God' (Gen 28:20-22, paraphrase).

Many Christians are just like that. God calls them to something great and glorious and they settle for something far, far inferior. God calls them to expend their energies in his work, but they waste their lives making money and seeking honour in this world. How few there are among God's children who recognize their high calling. Charles Spurgeon did. He exhorted his son, 'I should not like it, if you were meant by God to be a missionary, that you drivel down to a king or a millionaire. What are your kings and nobles compared with the dignity of winning souls to Christ?'

God's purpose for us—as for Jacob—extends far beyond mere physical blessings. His purpose is basically twofold—first that we might *manifest* the life of Christ to others; and secondly, that we might *minister* that life to others. This is the calling of the Christian—and there can be no greater calling on earth. Yet many Christians, like Jacob, don't recognize this—even some who are in Christian work. God gives them some spiritual gift or ability and soon they are so taken up with that that they go off on a tangent away from the central purpose of God for their lives. The gift becomes to them like a toy that a child plays around with. It fills their whole vision and they can never see anything beyond. How cleverly Satan has sidetracked them without their even realizing it!

Jacob could not take in the vastness of God's purpose for his life. He was satisfied with toys, when God wanted him to have heavenly riches. The result of such a narrow vision was that God's purposes for Jacob's life were delayed. God had to wait twenty years before Jacob was willing to take his mind away from the things of the world and set it on things above. How many Christians are frustrating and delaying God's glorious purposes for their lives, because of the narrowness of their vision, because they are taken up with lesser things than God's highest?

Paul was a different man. He could say at the end of his life that he had not been disobedient to the heavenly vision. On the Damascus Road, God had given him a vision of the great ministry he had for him—to open the blind eyes of people and to deliver them from Satan's power through the message of the gospel (Acts 26:16-18). And Paul never got bogged down with social work or anything lesser than that which God had called him to.

But Jacob did not respond like that, when God spoke to him. And so the sun set on his life and things grew darker and darker. But the wonderful thing is that God did not let Jacob go. God had promised him at Bethel, 'I will not leave you until I have fulfilled my promises to you'; and God kept his word. This is what encourages us—the perseverance of God with his stubborn children.

Divine discipline

In order to fulfil his promises to Jacob, God had to discipline him severely. And so we see from this point in the story up to the second meeting at Peniel twenty years of divine chastening in Jacob's life, in order that Jacob might come to the point where he would accept God's highest for his life.

First of all, God placed Jacob alongside another shrewd person. Laban was just as smart as Jacob, and as they lived together and came into close contact with each other, plenty of friction was generated and some of Jacob's rough edges were rubbed off. God knows whom to place us with in order to purge us of our crookedness. God measures out his disciplines to us according to our individual need; and he makes all things work together for our good, even when he places us alongside someone like Laban—provided we don't rebel against God's providences. Many people have learnt sanctification through God leading them to marry someone just like themselves. 'The sparks . . . fly when iron strikes iron' (Prov 27:17, TLB)—but it sharpens *both* pieces of iron!

Jacob, at last, began to reap what he had sown. All his life he had been cheating others. Now he got cheated himself. He went through his wedding ceremony, thinking he was marrying Rachel, but discovered the next morning that he had actually married Leah! He had met his match in Laban! He now got a taste himself of the bitter medicine that he had been doling out to others. God does not discipline without a purpose or arbitrarily. He knows what dosage each person needs and gives accordingly. With the pure God shows himself pure, and with the crooked he shows himself shrewd (Ps 18:26). He knows how to deal with every Jacob.

Jacob's problems were not yet over. After seven years of hard work, he obtained Rachel, only to discover that she was barren. God was merciful and finally gave Jacob a child through her, but even this brought no change in Jacob. He still couldn't trust God, but continued to scheme.

He next planned to rob Laban of his property. Jacob was clever. He knew all the tricks of the trade, and he knew how to get the best of Laban's cattle. How long God had to wait before Jacob learned to trust in him and forsake his own human ingenuity. It is the same problem that God has with many of his children today. He is not impressed by our cleverness. He waits for us to see the folly of all that, before he can use us to fulfil his will.

We find Jacob finally scheming to run away from Laban. He is tired of living with his father-in-law and wants to go away. But when he does run away, he finds that he has only jumped out of the frying pan into the fire. He hears that Esau is approaching him with a large army and that Laban is pursuing him from the rear. The one who tries to escape God's disciplines finds that it is not an easy task. If Jacob had left the matter in God's hands, God would have released him from Laban in his own way. But Jacob had not learned to trust God yet.

Finding himself hedged in and his life in danger, Jacob now begins to pray. He is quick to remind God of his promises made at Bethel (Gen 32:9-12). But prayer alone is not sufficient for Jacob. He has to scheme too. He thinks up a clever plan of saving part of his company at least—just in case God lets him down. How very much like those who talk of trusting God and 'living by faith', but all the time have some earthly source of security to fall back upon just in case faith alone does not work! Jacob was indeed very much like us.

And how often we find, as Jacob found when he met Esau, that our fears were unfounded, that there was no need to have schemed and worried and doubted God. Esau's heart was in God's hands, and God could turn it in whichever direction he chose. 'When a man is trying to please God, God makes even his worst enemies to be at peace with him' (Prov 16:7, TLB). God had told Jacob clearly that he would take care of him. But Jacob could not believe God's promise.

Jacob had twenty long and painful years of chastening under God's hand. We are not given all the details of what Jacob underwent—but he must have had a very rough time. It must have been physically exhausting too—working and sleeping out in the open, exposed to the sun and the dew and the rain. But all this discipline was necessary, in order to shatter Jacob's self-sufficiency and self-confidence. Only in later years, when he looked back, would he be able to appreciate what God took him through—not now. 'God's correction is always right and for our best good, that we may share his holiness. [But] being punished isn't enjoyable while it is happening—it hurts! But afterwards we can see the result, a quiet growth in grace and character' (Heb 12:10-11, TLB).

> With mercy and with judgement, my web of time he wove,
> And aye, the dews of sorrow were lustred by his love:
> I'll bless the Hand that guided, I'll bless the Heart that
>   planned,
> When throned where glory dwelleth in Immanuel's land.

THE SUN RISES

We have seen how the sun set upon Jacob's life and how

the darkness deepened through the ensuing twenty years. He was indeed an ordinary man just like us. And on such a man the sun rose one day. God met with him a second time and changed him into an 'Israel'—a prince of God.

Only God could have seen any good in such a useless person as Jacob, and followed after him patiently, without giving up hope. There we see the grace and greatness of our God. And this is what encourages us. In spite of all our self-centredness, God does not throw us on the scrap-heap. He is patient with us.

We may not believe in the doctrine of the perseverance of the saints, but we cannot but believe in the perseverance of God—'the undiscouraged perseverance of God with his elect', as J. Oswald Sanders has termed it. 'I will not leave you until I have done that which I have promised' was his promise to Jacob at Bethel—and his promise to us. How wonderful and how humbling it is to know the longsuffering of God in his dealings with us. If he were not like that, none of us would have any hope.

At Peniel God dealt a final blow on Jacob. He had been disciplining Jacob and breaking him, bit by bit, over the previous twenty years. But now the time had come to finish the work with one final blow. If God had not done that here, it might have taken twenty more years for the sun to rise on Jacob. God knows the right time to shatter our self-life once-and-for-all.

Blessed by God

And when God finally broke Jacob, *then* he was truly blessed. The record reads, 'And there he blessed him' (Gen 32:29). The word 'bless' is perhaps the most frequently used word in the prayers of Christians. But few understand its real meaning.

What is blessing? What was the blessing Jacob got? It

is described in verse 28 as 'power with God and with men' (AV). This is the blessing that we all need and that we should be seeking for. And this alone can make the sun to rise upon our lives. Nothing less than this is what God desires to give his people. Jesus referred to this blessing when he asked his disciples to wait in Jerusalem for the promise of the Father. He said, 'You shall receive power when the Holy Spirit has come upon you,' (Acts 1:8)—power with God and power with men. Jacobs would then be transformed into Israels. This was what made the sun to rise upon Peter's life and upon the lives of the other disciples, on the day of Pentecost.

And this alone can provide the answer to the crookedness of our self-life. It is not a question of reformation or of good resolutions or even of our determination. It is a question of the Holy Spirit filling us and governing and ruling our lives.

But how does the Spirit come? Always via the cross. When we are crucified, then and then alone can Christ live in us in his fullness. It was when Jesus was baptized, buried under the waters—symbolically accepting death to himself—that the Holy Spirit came upon him (Mt 3:16). It was when Jacob was broken that he was blessed. Calvary always precedes Pentecost. The rock must be smitten before the living waters can flow. The alabaster box must be broken before the odour of the ointment can fill the house. The Israelites had to go through the River Jordan (symbolizing death and burial) before they could enter Canaan (symbolizing life in the fullness of the Spirit). We find this truth throughout Scripture.

It would be dangerous for God to empower an unbroken man. It would be like giving a sharp knife to a six-month-old baby, or like putting your finger into 20,000 volts of electricity without proper insulation. God is careful. He does not desire the power of his Spirit to be manifested through those in whom self is still unbroken.

Jacob was now blessed by God himself. Earlier Isaac had laid his hands on Jacob and blessed him, when Jacob brought him the venison (Gen 27:23). But that had brought no change in Jacob's life. The real blessing came at Peniel. And this is the lesson we need to learn too. No man can ever give us this blessing. A man—even a saintly man like Isaac—may lay his hands on our head and pray for us. Yet we may get nothing. Only God can really empower us. When Isaac put his hands on Jacob's head, the sun merely *set* on Jacob's life. But when God blessed him, the sun *rose*. Power belongs to God and he is the only one who can ever give it to us.

The record says that God blessed Jacob *there* (Gen 32:29)—there, where Jacob fulfilled certain conditions and came to a certain point in his life. There were reasons why God blessed Jacob there at Peniel.

Alone with God

First of all, Jacob was blessed in the place where he was *alone* with God. He sent everyone else away and was alone (Gen 32:24). Twentieth-century believers find it difficult to spend much time alone with God. The spirit of the jet-age has got into most of us, and we are in a perpetual state of busyness. The trouble is not with our temperament or our culture. We just don't have our priorities right—that's all.

Jesus once said that the one thing needful for a believer was to sit at Jesus' feet and listen to him (Lk 10:42). But we don't believe that any longer and so suffer the disastrous consequences of disregarding Jesus' words. If we are always busy with our various activities and do not know what it is to get alone with God in prayer, we shall certainly not know God's power or blessing—his real power, I mean (not the cheap counterfeits that many are boasting of).

Broken by God

Secondly, Jacob was blessed in the place where he was *broken* completely. At Peniel, a Man wrestled with Jacob. God had been wrestling with Jacob for twenty years, but Jacob had refused to yield. God had tried to show him how everything he had put his hand to had gone wrong, despite his cleverness and his planning. But Jacob was still stubborn. Finally God struck Jacob's hip-socket so that his thigh was dislocated (Gen 32:25). The thigh is the strongest part of the body, and that was the part that God struck.

The strong-points in our life are what God seeks to shatter. Simon Peter had once thought that his strong point spiritually was his courage. Even if everyone else denied the Lord, he would never do so. And so God had to break him *there.* Peter denied the Lord before any of the others did, and not just once but three times, and that too when questioned by a weak little servant-girl! That was enough to shatter Peter. In the physical realm, Peter's strong point was fishing. If there was one thing he was an expert at, it was fishing. And so God broke him at that point as well. Peter fishes all night and gets nothing. And that too happened not just once but twice (Lk 5:4-8; Jn 21:3-8). God broke him at his strongest points to teach him his worthlessness.

It took three-and-a-half years for the disciples to learn that without Christ they could do nothing. It takes even longer for some of us. But it is only in the measure in which we learn the truth of those words that we can know God's power. When Peter was shattered at his strongest points—when he had been struck by God in his 'thigh'—then he was ready for Pentecost.

Moses' strong point was his leadership potential and his training in the best academies of Egypt. He thought he was well qualified to be the leader of the Israelites

(Acts 7:25). But God did not stand by him until, forty years later, shattered in his strongest points, he said, '[Lord,] I'm not the person for a job like that . . . I'm just not a good speaker. . . . Send someone else.' (Ex 3:11; 4:10, 13, TLB.) Then God took him up and used him in a big way. God has to wait till our self-sufficiency and our self-confidence are shattered, and we are broken and no longer think highly of ourselves or of our capabilities. Then he can commit himself to us unreservedly.

Hungry for God

Thirdly, Jacob was blessed in the place where he was earnest and *hungry for God.* 'I will not let you go,' he cries out, 'unless you bless me' (Gen 32:26). How God had waited for twenty long years to hear those words from Jacob. He, who had spent his life grabbing the birthright, women, money and property, now lets go of them all and grabs hold of God. This was the point towards which God had been working in Jacob's life all along. It must have delighted God's heart when Jacob at last lost sight of the temporal things of earth and longed and thirsted for God himself and for his blessing. We are told in Hosea 12:4 that Jacob wept and pleaded for a blessing that night at Peniel. What a different man he was that night compared with his earlier years when he desired only the things of this world. God's dealings with him at last bore fruit!

Before God blessed Jacob fully, he tested Jacob's earnestness. He said to Jacob, 'Let me go,' testing whether Jacob would be satisfied with what he had got or whether he would yearn for more. It was just as Elijah tested Elisha in later years. Elijah said, 'Let me go,' again and again, but Elisha refused to be shaken off—and so got a double portion of Elijah's spirit (2 Kings 2:1-12). Jesus, likewise, tested the two disciples walking to Emmaus (Lk 24:13-35). When they reached their house, Jesus made as though he would go further. But the two disciples would not let him go—and they got a blessing as a result.

God tests us too. He can never bless a man fully until the man is in dead earnest for God's best. We need to thirst like Jacob, saying, 'Lord, there is more to the Christian life than I've experienced thus far. I'm not satisfied. I want all your fullness at any cost.' Then God can lead us into his fullness.

Notice in the incident at Peniel that it was when Jacob was in a state of weakness (after his thigh had been dislocated) that he said, 'I will not let you go, God.' God could easily have left him and gone, but he didn't. For it is when a man is most weak in himself that he has greatest power with God. As the apostle Paul said, 'I am glad to boast about how weak I am; I am glad to be a living demonstration of *Christ's* power, instead of showing off my *own* power and abilities . . . for when I am weak, then I am strong' (2 Cor 12:9, 10, TLB, italics mine). God's power is most effectively demonstrated in human weakness. And so with Jacob, it is when he is defeated, broken and utterly weak, that God tells him, 'You have *prevailed*.' One would think that God should have said, 'You have at last been *defeated.*' But no. The word is, 'You have prevailed. From now on you will have power with God and with men' (Gen 32:28, paraphrase). We prevail when God has shattered us of our own strength and self-sufficiency. As the hymn says, 'Make me a captive, Lord, and then I shall be free.' This is the glorious paradox of the Christian life.

If ever there was a picture of weakness, surely it is seen in a man hanging helplessly on a cross. Beaten and buffeted and finally nailed to the cross, Christ died as a weak and exhausted man. But there the power of God was displayed in the overthrow of the devil and deliverance of men (Heb 2:14; Col 2:14-15). 'Christ crucified is . . . the power of God,' Paul wrote to the Corinthians. 'He was crucified in weakness, but lives by the power of God. For we are weak in him, but . . . shall live with him by the power of God' (1 Cor 1:23-24; 2 Cor 13:4). The Corinthian Christians were mistaking the gift of tongues for evidence of being endued with God's power, and so Paul had to correct their error. In essence he tells them, 'Brethren, the power of God is not seen in the gift of tongues. Thank God if you have that gift. But don't make any mistake. The power of God is manifested only in and via the cross. It is in human weakness that the might of God is seen.'

I remember hearing a certain servant of the Lord mentioning how God showed him the secret of spiritual power. He had sought God for spectacular manifestations for quite some time, and finally God asked him, 'How did you receive the forgiveness of your sins?' He replied, 'Lord, I recognized that I was the greatest sinner on earth and cried out for your mercy, and you forgave me.' 'Well,' God said, 'now recognize yourself to be the weakest man on earth and you shall have my power.' The way of the cross is the way of power. In the measure in which we walk that pathway we shall have God's power in our life, and people will be blessed through our life and our ministry. When the five loaves are broken, then and not before then will the multitude be fed.

Honest with God

Finally, Jacob was blessed in the place where he was *honest with God*. God asked him, 'What is your name?' Twenty years earlier, when his father had asked him the same question, he had lied and said, 'I am Esau' (Gen 27:19). But now he is honest. He says, 'Lord, I am Jacob'—or in other words, 'Lord, I am a grabber, a deceiver and a bargainer.' There was no guile in Jacob now. And so God could bless him.

When Jesus looked at Nathaniel, you remember what he said: 'Behold an Israelite [a true Israel, a genuine prince of God] in whom there is no "Jacob", no guile' (Jn 1:47). This is what God waits to see in us too. Only then can he empower us.

God blessed Jacob *there*—where he was honest, where he did not want to pretend any more, where he confessed, 'Lord I'm a hypocrite. There is sham and pretense in my life.' I tell you, it takes real brokenness for a man to say that from the depths of his heart. Many Christian leaders say words like that with false humility—to gain a reputation for being humble. I am not referring to that type of abomination. What I mean is an honesty that comes out of a truly broken and contrite heart. That is costly. There is so much guile in all of us. May God have mercy on us for pretending to be so sanctified when we are not. Let us covet sincerity and honesty and openness with all of our hearts, and then there will be no limit to God's blessing on our lives.

The ascending sun

Jacob was broken and thereby he became Israel. The sun rose on his life at last. This did not however, mean that Jacob had become perfect. There is no once-for-all experience that guarantees perfection. God had to discipline him further, for he still had plenty to learn. In Genesis 33 and 34 we read of some of Jacob's disobediences and blunders.

But the sun had risen on his life and he had entered into a new spiritual plane. The light had to increase in its brightness, no doubt, but that would come as the sun continued to ascend in the sky to its noon-day position. The Bible says, 'The path of the righteous is like the light of dawn, which shines brighter and brighter until full day' (Prov 4:18). So it was with Jacob and so it must be with us. If we submit to God's dealings with us, as Jacob finally did, the light of God will continuously increase upon our lives. And as it does so, the shadow of our self-life will continue to decrease until finally when the sun is overhead (when Christ returns), the shadows will disappear altogether and Christ will be all in all.

What was Jacob's testimony in later years, about his Peniel experience? He did *not* keep telling everyone that on such-and-such a date he had received a second blessing. No. His testimony was something quite different. In Hebrews 11 we are given an inkling as to what Jacob's testimony was. There we are given a record of some of the exploits of great men of faith in the Old Testament—splitting open seas, pulling down strong walls, shutting lions' mouths, raising the dead etc.. Jacob's name appears in the list too—and what do you think is recorded of him? He 'worshipped, leaning upon the top of his staff' (verse 21, AV). It looks quite incongruous to include something like that in a chapter full of spectacular events! What Jacob did certainly does not look like a 'miracle of faith'. But it was. It was perhaps a greater miracle than the other miracles recorded in the chapter. The staff had become necessary to Jacob, because his thigh had been dislocated at Peniel. Leaning upon that staff, he would always remember the miracle of grace that God had wrought in his life, in breaking his stubborn self-will, and now his leaning upon the staff symbolized to him his helpless, moment-by-moment dependence on his God. He worshipped God now as a broken man. He gloried in his weakness and his infirmity—and *that* was his daily testimony. So it was with the apostle Paul too. And so it has been with the great men and women of God in all ages. They rejoiced in their limitations and not in their achievements. What a lesson for proud, self-confident twentieth-century Christians!

Towards the end of his life, we see Jacob as a prophet. He prophesies concerning the future of his descendants (Gen 49). Only a man who has been under God's hand and who has submitted to the divine disciplines is qualified to prophesy. Jacob had learnt through experience. He was no seminary-qualified theoretician. He had been through the grill and qualified in God's University. He knew the secret counsels of God. Truly he was a prince of God. What a wonderful thing it is to be purged by God. What fruitfulness it results in!

Notice, finally, a word of encouragement that runs through the Bible. God calls himself, 'the God of Abraham, Isaac and Jacob' (not 'Israel', but 'Jacob'). This is wonderful indeed! He is the God of *Jacob.* He has linked his name with the name of Jacob, the grabber and the deceiver. This is our encouragement. Our God is the God of the warped personality and the difficult temperament. What meaning there is in the psalmist's words, 'The God of Jacob is our refuge' (Ps 46:7, 11). He is not only the Lord of hosts, but also the God of Jacob. Praise be to his name!

What God has begun in us he will complete. As perfect as was the work of the Father in creation and as perfect as was the work of the Son in our redemption, so perfect will the work of the Holy Spirit be in our sanctification. God is faithful. 'God who began the good work within [us] will keep right on helping [us] grow in grace until his task within [us] is finally finished on that day when Jesus Christ returns' (Phil 1:6, TLB). He will complete his work in us, as he completed his work in Jacob. But we must respond as Jacob did at Peniel. If however we do not co-operate with him, but frustrate his workings in us, we shall ultimately stand before him with the tragedy of a wasted, fruitless life. God wants us to be fruitful, but he won't compel us. He wants to transform us into the likeness of Christ, but he will never override our free will.

The pathway to the Christ-life is via the cross—being broken on it. What power is released when an atom is broken! What power can be released when a child of God is broken in God's hand!

May the Lord teach us this lesson and write it deeply on our hearts.

3. The pathway to the Christ-life (b) Being emptied

The way of the cross involves not only being broken but also being emptied. 'It is no longer I,' said Paul. He had allowed himself to be emptied of the 'I', so that Christ might live and rule in him. Even Jesus emptied himself when he came down from the throne of God to the awful depths of the cross (Phil 2:5-8). The cross will mean the same in our lives as it did to Jesus and to Paul.

We shall look at the life of Abraham in this chapter, to see what it means to be emptied. In James 2:23 Abraham is called 'the friend of God'. He was a type of those who, in the New Testament age, would be called the friends of God. Jesus told his disciples, just before he went to the cross, 'You are my *friends* if you obey me [as Abraham did]. I *no longer* call you slaves, for a master doesn't confide in his slaves; *now* you are my friends, proved by the fact that I have told you everything the Father told me' (Jn 15:14-15, TLB).

God calls us in this New Testament age to be not just his servants but his friends, entering into his secret counsels and understanding the hidden mysteries of his word. Abraham was such a friend. God revealed his secrets to him (Gen 18:17-19).

God blessed Abraham mightily. And we are told that 'all who trust in Christ [can] share the same blessing that Abraham received' (Gal 3:9, TLB). What was the blessing with which God blessed Abraham? God's promise to Abraham was, 'I will bless you' (Gen 12:2). We saw in the last chapter what it means to be blessed by God. But God's promise to Abraham did not end with 'I will bless you'. He went on to say, ' . . . and you will be a blessing to others.' This was God's full purpose for Abraham and is his purpose for us today. We are not only to be blessed but also to be channels through which that blessing is communicated to others. Galatians 3:14 makes it clear that the blessing of Abraham for us today is connected with the gift of the Holy Spirit. The Holy Spirit is the One who communicates the abundant life of Christ to us and then ministers that same life through us to others.

In James 2:21-23, where Abraham is called God's friend, two incidents from Abraham's life are mentioned:

(a) His believing God when God told him that he would have a son (verse 23—referring to Gen 15:6)

(b) His offering up Isaac when God asked him to (verse 21—referring to Gen 22:2, 9-10).

These two incidents described in Genesis 15 and 22 are brought together by James when referring to Abraham's being called God's friend. The chapters in Genesis describe two important periods in Abraham's life. Moreover, in these two chapters, we find the first occurrences in the Bible of two important words—in Genesis 15:6 the word *believe* and in Genesis 22:5 the word *worship*. There is such a thing as the law of first mention in Scripture. This simply means that the first time an important word occurs in the Bible, there is a significance about the context in which the word occurs. So these two passages of Scripture have much to teach us concerning the true meanings of faith and worship. And these were the two lessons that Abraham had to learn—what it meant to believe God and what it meant to worship him. Both of these are possible only as we accept the cross as the instrument of our self-emptying.

Abraham had to learn that trusting God meant not merely intellectual belief, but also being emptied of self-sufficiency and self-dependence.

In Genesis 15 (where the word 'believe' occurs in verse 6), the paragraph begins with the words, 'After these things . . . (verse 1). The previous chapter, to which that phrase refers, indicates that it was a time of great triumph in Abraham's life. With 318 untrained servants he had gone out and defeated the armies of four kings. And then at the end of all that, he had conducted himself so nobly before the king of Sodom, refusing to take any reward for his efforts. God had helped him marvellously on both these occasions. Now, in the hour of his triumph, it was so easy for Abraham to feel self-sufficient.

At such a time, God spoke to Abraham and told him that he was going to have a son. And not only that, but God also said that through that son would come a seed that would be like the stars of the heaven for number. It looked almost impossible, but Abraham believed the Lord (Gen 15:6). The Hebrew word translated 'believe' here is *aman*, which is allied to the word we use at the end of our prayers—'Amen'. It means, 'It shall be so'. When God told Abraham that he was going to have a son, he replied with an 'Amen', meaning in essence, 'Lord, I don't know how this is going to take place, but since you have said it, I believe it shall be so.'

God's promise looked difficult to fulfil because Sarah was barren. Of course, Abraham himself was still fertile. So there was some hope. In other words, the promise was not exactly *impossible,* but certainly *difficult.*

Helping God out of a tight spot

After Abraham heard God's promise, he must have reasoned with himself and said, 'Well, I suppose I should help God out in this situation, since Sarah is barren.' And so he readily accepted Sarah's suggestion to unite with Hagar his maid. He sincerely desired to help God. He felt that God was in a tight spot; having made a promise which could not, humanly speaking, be fulfilled. God's reputation was at stake. And so, to save God out of this awkward situation, Abraham united with Hagar and produced Ishmael! But God rejected this seed of Abraham as unacceptable, for it was the product of man's self-effort.

So much of the motivation for Christian work in our day, alas, arises out of the same carnal reasoning that Abraham had. Believers are told that God is depending on their efforts and that if they let him down, his purposes will fail. Things apparently have not worked out as God planned and as a result he is in a tight spot now! Some exhortations to Christian service give us the impression that the Almighty is now at his wit's end and is desperately in need of our help!

We know that God uses human agency for the outworking of his purposes. He has voluntarily accepted this limitation because he wants us to have the privilege of co-operating with him in his work. But that certainly does not mean that if we disobey God, his work will remain undone. No. He is sovereign. There is certainly a work for Jesus that we can do; but if we don't do it, he will just pass us by and take up someone else to do the job—and we shall miss the privilege of being God's co-workers. Mere men are not going to hinder God from carrying out his programme.

God can carry on his work very well without our help. We need to recognize that fact. If our service for God originates out of any idea that we are helping God out of a tight spot, we shall only produce unacceptable Ishmaels. That service which has its roots in human energy and fleshly wisdom and in human ability and natural talents (even at their very best) is totally unacceptable to God. Ishmael may be very smart and impressive. Abraham may even cry out to God saying, 'O that Ishmael might live in thy sight!' (Gen 17:18). But God's answer is to this effect: 'No. He was born through your strength, Abraham. So I cannot accept him, however good he may be.'

And so with service that originates from ourselves. If there is any human explanation for our Christian service—if it is merely the result of excellent theological training that our sharp minds have assimilated, or made possible because we have access to enough money to support ourselves in Christian work—then however impressive our work may appear in the eyes of men, it will be burnt up in the day of testing as wood, hay and straw. That day will reveal the multitude of 'Ishmaels' produced by well-meaning Christians who were never emptied of their self-sufficiency. The only work that will abide for eternity is that which is produced in humble dependence upon the power of God's Holy Spirit. May God help us to learn that lesson now, instead of regretting at Christ's judgement seat.

Works of faith

Our self-life is so subtle and deceitful that it can enter the very sanctuary of God and attempt to serve him. We have to watch that—and put self to death even when it seeks to serve God.

God's work has to be a work of *faith*—that is, one that originates in man's helpless dependence upon God. It is therefore not a question of how effective our work is in the eyes of men or in our own eyes. The important question is whether the work is the result of the Holy Spirit's working or of our own. God is not so much interested in how much is done, as in the question of whose power has energized the work. Was the work done by the power of money and intellectual ability, or by the power of the Holy Spirit? This is the real test of a spiritual work, a work of faith. In other words, God is more interested in quality than in quantity. God's true work carries on today, as of old, not by human power or might, but by the power of the Holy Spirit (Zech 4:6). We forget this truth to our own peril.

Man's extremity—God's opportunity

Isaac, unlike Ishmael, was not the product of Abraham's strength, for Abraham had become sterile by then. Isaac was born through God strengthening impotent Abraham. This is the type of service that lasts for eternity. One Isaac is worth a thousand Ishmaels. All Ishmaels will have to be cast out finally. Abraham could keep Ishmael for some time, but finally God asked him to cast him out (Gen 21:10-14). Only Isaac could remain with him. There is a spiritual lesson here. That service which is the result of God working through us will alone remain for eternity. Everything else will be burnt up. You may have heard the saying, 'Only one life, it will soon be past; only what's done for Christ will last.' It would be more accurate to say, 'Only what is done in the will of God will last' (see 1 Jn 2:17). Paul lived and laboured in God's power (Gal 2:20; Col 1:29). Hence his life and labours were so effective. He lived by faith and he worked by faith.

In Genesis 16:16 we read that Abraham was 86 years old when Hagar bore Ishmael. In the very next verse we read that Abraham was 99 years old when God appeared to him again. We see here a gap of thirteen years. Those were years when God waited for Abraham to become impotent. God could not fulfil his promise till Abraham had become impotent. This is God's way with all his servants. He cannot work through them till they recognize their impotence. And in some case he has to wait for many years.

Abraham needed to learn what it really meant to trust God. He had to learn that *it was only when he became impotent that he could truly exercise faith*. In Romans 4:19-21 we read that although Abraham knew that his body was impotent to produce a son, yet that did not worry him. He was strong in faith and glorified God by believing that God was well able to perform what he had promised. He did not waver in unbelief, for his feet stood firm on the rock of God's word to him. But when could Abraham exercise such faith? Only when he had come to an end of all confidence in his own ability. We too can exercise real faith only when we reach that state of utter helplessness. This is God's way, so that no flesh may ever glory in his presence.

This does *not* however mean that we do nothing. No. God does not want us to be reduced to a state of inactivity. That is the other extreme of error. God *used* Abraham to produce Isaac. God didn't do it all by himself, for Isaac was not born apart from Abraham fulfilling the father's part. No. But there was a difference between the birth of Ishmael and the birth of Isaac. In both cases Abraham was the father. But in the first case it was in dependence upon his own strength; in the second it was in dependence upon the power of God. That was the difference—and what a vital difference!

No confidence in the flesh

At the end of the thirteen years of waiting, when God appeared to Abraham, he gave him the covenant of circumcision (Gen 17:11). Circumcision involved a cutting-off and a casting-off of human flesh. It symbolized a casting off of all confidence in self. In Philippians 3:3

Paul explains what circumcision means. He says there, 'We are the true circumcision . . . who put no confidence in the flesh.'

Notice that *in the very same year* that Abraham obeyed God and circumcised himself, Isaac was conceived (cf. Gen 17:1 and 21:5). There is a lesson for us to learn here. God waits until we learn to put no confidence in ourselves and our abilities. And when we finally come to the place where we realize that it is impossible for us in ourselves to serve God and to please him (Rom 8:8), and when we trust God to work through us, then he takes us up and does an eternal work through us. At the age of 85 the birth of a child to Abraham looked *difficult*. By the time he was 99 and impotent, that which had been difficult had now become *impossible.* Then God acted. Someone has said that in a true work of God, there are three stages—Difficult, Impossible and Done! Human wisdom finds it difficult to follow such reasoning, for spiritual truth is foolishness to the natural mind. But this is God's way.

No flesh will ever be able to glory in God's presence, either now or in eternity. God is working to the point where finally Christ will have the pre-eminence in all things (Col 1:18). If there is going to be some work in heaven which lasts for eternity, which has been done by human ingenuity and cleverness, then all through eternity some man will be able to take the credit for it. But God is going to make sure that will not be so. All that ministers to human glory will be burnt up at the judgement seat of Christ. Here on earth men may receive the credit for something they do, but that will all be reduced to ashes before we reach the shores of eternity. One of these days, God will gather up all things in Christ and then throughout eternal ages Christ alone will have the pre-eminence.

The biography of one of God's saints records that there

was a time in her life when after some years of serving God she came to a place of dissatisfaction with the results of her labours. She was born again, but she realized that she needed to be filled with the Holy Spirit as well. And so she sought God's face earnestly for this. One day, while in prayer, she saw a vision of a hand holding a bundle of dirty rags. A voice said, 'This is the result of all your service for me thus far.' She was surprised. Here she was, a born-again and consecrated child of God. Surely this was not a picture of *her* labours. But the Lord showed her that it was her self-life that she had consecrated to God and that self could produce only dirty rags. And then the Lord spoke to her that she needed to be *crucified*. This was difficult for her to accept initially. But she did. And as a result, rivers of living water began to flow through her life, bringing blessing and refreshment to thousands in many parts of the world. Truly she inherited Abraham's blessing—and people of many nations were blessed through her.

Self *must* be crucified, before there can be service that pleases God. We may serve God with all our hearts and then say, 'Lord, please accept these Ishmaels that I have produced.' But God will say no! He will say no now and he will say no in eternity.

Dependence on the Holy Spirit

Let us test ourselves in one area—the area of prayer. Do we really know what it is to pray what the Bible calls 'the prayer of faith'? It is only when we come to an end of ourselves that we can do that. For, as it has been said, prayer is simply confessing our helplessness to God. There is no credit in uttering beautiful, eloquent and impressive prayers. Such ordinary praying can be done by anyone—even by a heathen. But the prayer of faith can come only from one who has recognized his impotence and utter helplessness without God. This is what it means to 'pray in the Spirit' (Eph 6:18); and that is the only type of prayer that brings an answer. As someone has said, what we need in our day is not more prayer but more *answered* prayer. Let us not fool ourselves, like the heathen, that God is pleased by our much praying. No. Prayer has no value before God if it does not arise out of a recognition of our own impotence.

So little of Christian work today is a work of *faith*. We have so many electronic gadgets and other similar aids to help us in our service for the Lord, that many of us are all unconsciously depending on them rather than on the Lord. Apparently you don't need to be filled with the Holy Spirit, these days, to serve the Lord. All you need is a tape-recorder, a projector with a few Christian films, audio-visual aids, and some rich businessmen to provide financial support. If added to these you also have a dynamic personality and eloquence, or a trained singing voice, you can go out and 'win souls for Christ'! How far 'evangelical Christianity' has drifted from the faith of the apostles! What a tragedy that the techniques of the business world are brought into the sanctuary of God. Let us never be fooled by the apparent success of these methods. We can accumulate statistics of our 'conversions', but we shall realize in eternity that they were spurious. Heaven does not rejoice over our labours, because we have not delivered souls from their self-centredness but merely entertained them and given them a good time.

God's way has not changed. Even today, we need to be emptied of our self-sufficiency and filled with the Spirit of God, if we are to produce 'Isaacs' that please God. The Bible says, 'Cursed be the man who depends on man and who makes his self-sufficiency the arm on which he leans . . . for he shall be like a barren tree' (Jer 17:5-6, paraphrase). Such a man may give the appearance of fruitfulness to others, but he will stand in eternity like a barren tree, for his work originated in himself and in dependence on human energies and human resources. On the other hand it says, 'Blessed is the man who trusts in the Lord and has made the Lord his hope and confidence. He is like a tree planted along a riverbank, with its roots reaching deep into the water . . . its leaves stay green and it goes right on producing all its luscious fruit' (Jer 17:7-8, TLB).

To change the illustration to the one found in 1 Corinthians 3:10-15, with what are we building? Wood, hay and straw; or gold, silver and precious stones? One ounce of gold is worth more than a ton of straw after the fire has done its work. Only genuine works of faith will abide in that day of testing.

An end of ourselves

In Edith Schaeffer's book, *L'Abri,* she recounts how God brought her husband Francis Schaeffer and his co-workers again and again to a point of utter helplessness. More than once they found that there was no way out of the impasse. The enemies of the gospel almost triumphed at many a point. In their impotence, they looked to God to work on their behalf. And he did—not just once or twice but repeatedly.

It is not the size of a work that impresses God. The world looks for size and numbers. But God is looking for works of faith—even if they be the size of mustard seeds.

And so, when God brings us to an end of ourselves, hedging us in on every side and shattering our hopes, let us take heart! He is preparing us for greater usefulness by bringing us first to the place of impotence. He's equipping us to produce Isaacs.

This was how Jesus prepared his apostles for his service. What do you think was the purpose of his training them for three-and-a-half years? They were not being coached to write scholarly theses that would earn each of them a doctorate in theology. That's how some people today feel they can be equipped to serve the Lord. But Jesus didn't train his apostles for that. None of the twelve disciples (except perhaps Judas Iscariot!) would have qualified for a basic theological degree (by our standards), even if they had tried. Jesus trained them to learn one lesson primarily—that without him they could do nothing (Jn 15:5). And I tell you, a man who has learned that lesson is worth more than a hundred theological professors who haven't learnt that lesson.

Total dependence upon God is the mark of the true servant of God. It was true even of the Lord Jesus Christ, when he was on earth, as the Servant of Jehovah. In a prophetic reference to him in Isaiah 42:1, God says, 'Behold my servant, *whom I uphold.*' He does not stand in his own strength; he is upheld by God. Because Christ emptied himself in this way, God put his Spirit upon him, as the verse goes on to say. Indeed, it is only on those who have come to an end of themselves, and who have emptied themselves of self-confidence and self-sufficiency, that God pours out his Spirit.

Look at some of the remarkable statements that Jesus made, which clearly show how emptied of self he was:

> 'The Son can do nothing of his own accord' (Jn 5:19).
> 'I can do nothing on my own authority' (Jn 5:30; 8:28).
> 'I have not spoken on my own authority; the Father who sent me has himself given me commandment what to say' (Jn 12:49).
> 'The words that I say to you I do not speak on my own authority' (Jn 14:10).

Amazing! The perfect, sinless Son of God lived by faith. Emptied of all dependence upon his own self, he depended entirely on his Father. It is thus that God calls us to live too.

When we are self-sufficient, *we try to use God* to help us serve him. But when we are emptied, *God can use us.* A. B. Simpson, that great man of God who founded the Christian and Missionary Alliance, tells us how he learnt this lesson in his own life. As a young pastor he struggled to serve God with his own energies, until he was broken down in health. Finally he met with God in such a way that it changed his whole outlook on Christian service. *He* had been using God. Henceforth he would let *God* use him. He expressed his experience in these words:

Once it was the blessing, now it is the Lord;
Once it was the feeling, now it is His Word;
Once His gift I wanted, now the Giver own;
Once I sought for healing, now Himself alone.

Once 'twas painful trying, now 'tis perfect trust;
Once a half salvation, now the uttermost;
Once 'twas ceaseless holding, now He holds me fast;
Once 'twas constant drifting, now my anchor's cast.

Once 'twas busy planning, now 'tis trustful prayer;
Once 'twas anxious caring, now He has the care;
Once 'twas what I wanted, now what Jesus says;
Once 'twas constant asking, now 'tis ceaseless praise.

Once it was my working, His it hence shall be;
Once I tried to use Him, now He uses me;
Once the power I wanted, now the Mighty One;
Once for self I laboured, now for Him alone.

Once I hoped in Jesus, now I know He's mine;
Once my lamps were dying, now they brightly shine;
Once for death I waited, now His coming hail;
And my hopes are anchored safe within the veil.

All in all forever, Jesus, will I sing,
Everything in Jesus, and Jesus everything.

This is what it means to trust God. And this was the first lesson that Abraham had to learn.

WORSHIPPING GOD

The second lesson that Abraham had to learn was the true meaning of worship. If trusting God means to be *emptied of self-confidence and self-sufficiency,* worshipping God means to be *emptied of everything* (including one's possessions).

As in Genesis 15, in Genesis 22 also, the paragraph begins with the phrase 'After these things . . .'. Here too, as we look at the circumstances that immediately precede this hour of testing, we find Abraham in a triumphant position. The heathen had come to him and said, in effect, 'Abraham, we've been watching your life and we know that God is with you in all that you do' (Gen 21:22). No doubt they had heard of the miraculous way in which Sarah had conceived and were convinced that God was with this family. Ishmael having been sent away, Isaac was now the darling of Abraham's heart. Abraham stood in grave danger, at such a time, of losing his first love and devotion for God. And so God tested him again, and told him to offer up Isaac as a sacrifice.

Sacrifice and worship

Have we ever heard God calling us to hard and difficult tasks like that? Or do we only hear him comforting us with promises all the time? Oswald Chambers has said that if we have never heard God speaking a hard word to us, it is doubtful whether we have ever *really* heard God at all. It is very easy for our carnal minds to imagine that God is speaking to us with comforting promises all the time. Because we do not like the hard way, we can be deaf to God's voice when he calls us to a difficult task.

But Abraham had ears to hear, and a heart that was willing to obey anything that God commanded. He rose up early the next morning and went forth to obey God (Gen 22:3). The record does not tell us what the old patriarch went through, during the previous night, after God had spoken to him. I am sure he did not sleep that night. He must have kept awake and gone and looked at his beloved son again and again; and the tears must have rolled down his cheeks as he thought of what he had to do to him. How difficult it must have been for Abraham to offer up the son of his old age. But he was willing to obey God at any cost. Fifty years or so earlier he had put his hand to the plough when God called him in Ur; and he would not now look back.

Keep me from looking back.
The handles of my plough with tears are wet,
The shears with rust are spoiled, and yet, and yet,
My God! My God! Keep me from turning back.

There were no complaints and no questions. Abraham did not say, 'Lord, I've been so faithful already. Why do you ask this hard thing also?' Neither did he say, 'Lord, I've already sacrificed so much—much more than all those around me. Why do you call me to sacrifice more?' Many believers often compare the sacrifices they have made with those that others have made. And they hesitate when God calls them to go further than others around them. But not so Abraham. There was no limit to his obedience and no end to his willingness to sacrifice for his God. No wonder he became the friend of God.

There was faith in Abraham's heart as he went up to sacrifice Isaac, that God would somehow raise his son from the dead. Hebrews 11:19 tells us that God had already given Abraham a foretaste of resurrection-power in his own body and in Sarah's, through the birth of Isaac. Surely it would be no problem for such a God to bring back to life an Isaac who was slain on the altar. And so Abraham tells his servants when leaving them at the foot of Mount Moriah, 'I and the lad will go yonder and worship, and [we will both] come [back] again to you' (Gen 22:5). That was a word of faith. He believed that Isaac would come back with him.

Notice too that he tells his servants, 'We are going to *worship* God.' He is not complaining that God is requiring too much from him, neither is he boasting about the marvellous sacrifice that he is about to make for God. No. Abraham did not belong to that number who keep drawing the attention of others subtly to the sacrifices that they have made in their lives for God. Abraham said he was going to *worship* his God. And there we understand something of the real meaning of worship.

Remember how Jesus once said, 'Abraham rejoiced to see my day: and he saw it and was glad' (Jn 8:56, AV). Surely it must have been here on Mount Moriah that Abraham saw the day of Christ. In prophetic vision, the aged patriarch saw in his own action a picture (faint though it was) of that day when God the Father himself would lead his only begotten Son up Calvary's hill, and offer him up as a sacrifice for the sins of mankind. And that day on Mount Moriah, Abraham knew something of what it would cost the heart of God to save a wayward world. He came into a place of intimate fellowship with the heart of God that morning. Yes, he worshipped God—not just with beautiful words and hymns, but through costly obedience and sacrifice.

A deep and intimate knowledge of God can come only through such obedience. We may accumulate plenty of accurate theological information in our minds, but real spiritual knowledge can come only when a man has given up everything to God. There is no other way.

The Giver or his gift?

Abraham was being tested here as to whether he loved the Giver or his gifts more. Isaac was no doubt the gift of God, but Abraham was in danger of having an inordinate affection for his son. Isaac was beginning to become an idol who would cloud Abraham's spiritual vision. And so God intervened to save Abraham from such a tragedy. In *The Pursuit of God*, A. W. Tozer speaks of the blessedness of possessing nothing. God was teaching Abraham on Mount Moriah this blessedness of being emptied of everything and possessing nothing. Before that day, Abraham had held Isaac with a possessive spirit. But after he laid his son on that altar and gave him up to God, he never *possessed* Isaac again. Oh yes, God gave Isaac back to Abraham, and Abraham had him in his house. But he never possessed Isaac as his own again. From then on Isaac was God's. And Abraham held Isaac as a steward holds the property of his master. In other words, he had Isaac, but he never again possessed him.

This is to be our attitude to all the things of this world. We can have them and use them. But we are never to cling to any one of them. Everything we own should have been placed on the altar and given completely to God. We must possess nothing. We can then keep only that which God gives back to us from the altar—and we are to keep even these things only as stewards. Only then can we truly *worship* God. This is the pathway to the glory of the Christ-life.

This principle does not apply to material things alone. It applies to spiritual gifts as well. It is possible for us to hold even the gifts of the Holy Spirit in a possessive way. Was not Isaac the gift of God? Why couldn't Abraham hold on to him then? To have to send away Ishmael was understandable, because he was not the promised seed.

But Isaac's case was different. He was God's gift, produced in God's strength. Why should Abraham have to give him up as well?

And so we may argue too. We can understand the need to give up our attachment to the things of the world. But surely, we feel, we can hold on to the gifts that God himself has given us. But God says, 'No. Lay even your spiritual gifts (which I have given you) on the altar and give them back to me, lest they fill your life and cloud out your vision of me, the Giver.' God would have us delivered from any inordinate attachment to even the most sacred gifts of the Spirit that he has given us. He wants us to sacrifice even the Isaacs that we have received from him in answer to our fasting and prayer, and not cling to any one of them. Is this not what many good believers in our day have failed to see? They have given up their Ishmaels but not their Isaacs. The gift that God gave them they have begun to use to glorify themselves—like the prodigal son, who took his father's gifts and spent them on himself.

What is it that fills our vision—our gifts and our ministry, or the Giver himself? This is what we need to ask ourselves constantly. We are most in danger when God has blessed us much and used us greatly. It is so easy at such times to lose the vision of God. We need to go back to the altar on Mount Moriah again and again. We need to pray like Jim Eliot did, 'Lord, deliver me from clutching and grabbing. Give me the open palm to receive the nail of Calvary.'

This is true worship—where the Giver himself fills our hearts and our vision. Then we can safely use the gifts. Otherwise we shall abuse God's gifts and prostitute them to selfish uses. Why is there such misuse of the gifts of the Holy Spirit in our day? Is not the reason here—that the gifts have so filled the vision of many Christians that they have lost sight of the Giver?

Something that costs us everything

Abraham's devotion was tested that day when God asked him for Isaac. Had God asked Abraham for 10,000 sheep or for 5,000 rams, that would have been far easier for Abraham to offer. But one Isaac cost him everything, and he decided to offer nothing less than what God asked for. Abraham would have been able to echo the words that David said years later, 'I will not offer . . . to the Lord my God [that] which costs me nothing' (2 Sam 24:24). Yes, true worship involves our offering to God that which costs us everything.

It is more than mere coincidence that it was on this very spot on Mount Moriah, where Abraham offered Isaac, that the threshing-floor of Araunah the Jebusite was also located, where David said those words just quoted. And finally, Solomon built his famous temple on this very spot too (2 Chron 3:1). God ordained his house to be built in the place where two of his servants (Abraham and David) had made costly sacrifices. That was where the fire fell from heaven and that was where the glory of God was seen (2 Chron 7:1). It is even so today. God builds his true church and manifests his power and glory where he finds men and women who are willing to deny themselves and offer to him that which costs them everything.

Does our Christianity cost us something? Is our service for God an easygoing, cheap thing that does not cost us much travail of soul? Does our prayer-life cost us something? Or have we drawn a limit to the sacrifices we are willing to make for God? Do we look for ease and comfort? Or are we still expecting the fire to fall and the glory of God to be seen in our lives? Let us not deceive ourselves. The fullness of the Holy Spirit can result only from a wholehearted giving up of ourselves to God.

The way of the cross *is* difficult. How difficult it must

have been for Abraham to face the thought of slaying his son himself! It is not easy for us to see our children suffering as a result of the stand we have taken for God. That can be very costly. But blessed are we if we are willing even for that. God is no man's debtor. If we have honoured him, he will certainly honour us; and we shall find our children following God too, as Isaac followed in Abraham's footsteps. Isaac's willingness to be tied to the altar and slain was itself an indication of his devotion to his father's God. He was a strong and able-bodied young man, and his aged father could never have tied him to the altar if he himself had not been willing. But Isaac had seen the reality of God in his father's life, and so he too was willing to submit to anything that God desired.

On the other hand, many believers have often lowered their high standards and compromised Christian principles, for the sake of some material advantage for their children—only to see their children growing up to break their hearts and live for the world. Oh the tragedy of it!

Heaven's greatest rewards are reserved for those who have followed in Abraham's footsteps, and who like him have not withheld anything from God, whatever the cost.

I remember hearing the story of a young American couple who went to China as missionaries, before the communists took over that land. They asked their mission board to assign them to some virgin territory that had not yet been evangelized. Accordingly, they were posted to a little village in the interior, near Tibet. They laboured faithfully there for seven years, but did not see a single soul saved. God then gave them a gift of a baby daughter. And as that daughter grew up, they saw a miracle taking place before their eyes. They taught their little girl Bible verses and choruses in the local language, and she in turn taught them to the children with whom she played. Those children went home and taught these verses to their parents. Soon one person was converted to Christ.

This missionary couple continued to labour there for another fourteen years (making a total of twenty-one years) without a furlough, and in that period seven more souls were saved. (God doesn't measure success by statistics as men do. This couple had spent twenty-one years to show eight souls the way to eternal life. Surely their reward will be great when Christ returns.) At the end of those twenty-one years, one day the father noticed a patch on the hand of his fourteen-year-old daughter. They took her to a doctor who told them that the girl had contracted leprosy. It broke their hearts to think of what their child had to suffer because of their devotion to God and to his call. The mother and daughter travelled back to America for treatment. But the man himself stayed on in China. When asked why he did not go back to America with his family, he replied, 'I would have liked to have gone home with my family. But back there in my mission station, there are eight souls who need to be instructed and fed. If someone else replaces me, it will take years before they develop confidence in him. And so I feel I should go back.' It cost that family everything they had, to serve God.

So many believers who have so much give so little to God. But a few who have so little give so much. And it is through this small and faithful remnant that God builds his church. The kingdom of God does not come through spectacular outward show, but through men of God such as that missionary. Some of these men may never even be heard of on earth. But they shall shine as stars in eternity.

The apostle Paul could have chosen an easy life, when he was saved on the Damascus Road. He could have settled down to a comfortable life as a Christian businessman in Antioch or in Tarsus. But he didn't do that. He went out to serve God and endured hardship. He got 195 stripes on his back, he was stoned and suffered shipwreck, and faced many dangers in his service for God. If we were to ask him why he endured all that, he'd say, 'When I gave my life to Jesus, I determined that I would never offer to him any service that cost me nothing.'

The Moravian brethren, two hundred years ago, formed one of the greatest missionary movements that the world has ever seen. Two of their number heard of a slave colony in the West Indies and voluntarily sold themselves as slaves for the rest of their lives, in order to get into that island to preach the gospel to the slaves there. Two others heard of a leper-colony in Africa where no one was allowed to enter and return, for fear that the disease might spread. They volunteered to go into that leper colony for the rest of their lives, in order to present Christ to the inmates of the colony. These Moravian brethren knew what it was to worship God, by offering him that which cost them everything.

How shallow and superficial our lives and labours are, compared with those of men like these. How much has it cost us to serve God—in terms of loss of money, comfort, reputation, honour and health? Do we realize that we do not really know what it is to worship God if our Christianity has not cost us everything that this world counts dear. Those who serve God wholeheartedly, giving up everything for him, are the only ones who will have no regret in eternity. The Lord is calling today for those who will follow him in the pathway of the cross—being emptied of everything.

So send I you—to labour unrewarded,
To serve unpaid, unloved, unsought, unknown,
To bear rebuke, to suffer scorn and scoffing,
So send I you—to toil for Me alone.

So send I you—to bind the bruised and broken,
O'er wandering souls to work, to weep, to wake,

To bear the burdens of a world aweary,
So send I you—to suffer for My sake.

So send I you—to loneliness and longing,
With heart a-hungering for the loved and known;
Forsaking home and kindred, friend and dear one,
So send I you—to know My love alone.

So send I you—to leave your life's ambitions,
To die to dear desire, self-will resign,
To labour long and love when men revile you,
So send I you—to lose your life in Mine.

So send I you—to hearts made hard by hatred,
To eyes made blind because they will not see;
To spend though it be blood—to spend and spare not
So send I you—to *taste of Calvary.*

'As my Father hath send me, so send I you.'

This is the way of power. And we need to be reminded of it again in a day when many think that there are short-cuts and once-for-all experiences that guarantee spiritual power. The way of the cross alone is the way of power. Jesus steadfastly set his face to go to the cross. What about us? We shall face this choice daily. If we are looking for three easy steps to the victorious life, then the Bible has no message for us. But if we are willing to pay the price of denying ourselves and taking up our cross *daily* and following Jesus, then we shall indeed know the power of the Spirit of God resting upon us for our life and service.

4. The beauty of the Christ-life

Christ came to give us 'beauty for ashes'—the beauty of his own divine life for the ashes of our self-life. We have seen some of the characteristics of the self-life. And we have also seen that the way of the cross—being broken and being emptied—is the only pathway that can lead us out of the darkness of our self-life into the full glory of the Christ-life. One day, when Christ returns and all shadows disappear, the glory will shine undimmed on all who have walked this pathway. But even now, here on earth, our lives can reflect something of that glory. This is why God has given us his Holy Spirit. He wants to fill our lives. The beauty of the Christ-life is brought to us through the fullness of the Holy Spirit.

Before considering the characteristics of a Spirit-filled person, there are a few common misunderstandings concerning the Holy Spirit and his ministry that need to be cleared up.

The sovereignty of the Spirit

First of all, we must remember that the Holy Spirit is sovereign and works in varied ways. Jesus said, 'Just as you can hear the wind but can't tell where it comes from or where it will go next, so it is with the Spirit' (Jn 3:8 TLB). You can't control the wind—either its speed or its direction. So too with the Holy Spirit. And yet many believers think that they can control him and make him work according to their rules and patterns. When the second Person of the Trinity was here on earth, the Pharisees tried to tie him down with their petty rules and traditions. But he refused to be locked up in their watertight compartments. The descendants of the Pharisees in evangelical Christianity are today trying to tie down the third Person of the Trinity. But he refuses to work according to man-made patterns. He blows where he wishes. We can hear the sound of his working, but he will not be controlled or directed by us. We cannot say that he should work in the same way in other lives as he has worked in ours; neither should we expect him to work today in the same way as he worked in days past. No. He is sovereign. The best thing that we can do is to set our face towards the direction in which the wind is blowing and to let that wind carry us along. The Holy Spirit cannot be tied down in any doctrinal compartments of any denomination. We shall find that he surprises us by the way he works. Both Pentecostals and non-Pentecostals need to recognize this.

The Holy Spirit may at times manifest himself like a whirlwind. There may be deep stirrings of the emotions and even physical reactions too. We must be willing to accept this. God spoke to Job out of a whirlwind (Job 38:1).

But we also need to remember that the Spirit may at times blow like a gentle breeze. When Elijah heard the whirlwind, it says that God was *not* in the wind (1 Kings 19:11). No. Every stirring of the emotions is not from God. And so we must be careful. To Elijah, God spoke in a gentle whisper (1 Kings 19:12).

The Holy Spirit does not always blow like a tornado. Sometimes he does, but not always. We should not expect him to blow like a whirlwind all the time in everyone's life, just because he did so once in someone's life. Equally, we should not expect him to blow always like a gentle breeze. We do need his blowing as a tornado upon many of our churches today, to uproot the things that are dishonouring to Christ.

The wrapping should never be mistaken for the gift. The Holy Spirit himself is the Gift of the risen Lord to his church. When he falls upon people, it may be with shouts of Hallelujah, tears of joy and the gift of tongues, or it may be quietly, silently and without much emotion. Temperaments vary, and the Spirit of God (unlike many Christians) is willing to adapt himself to each temperament. It is foolish therefore to expect that others should receive the Gift in the same wrapping in which we received him—whether spectacular or commonplace. Only babies are taken up with the tissue-paper in which a gift comes to them. Mature men recognize that the gift itself is more important than the wrapping. The apostle Paul was converted through a vision of Jesus. But he did not preach that all needed a similar vision before they could be saved. No. He recognized that it was the inner reality that mattered, in whatever wrapping it might come. So too with the fullness of the Holy Spirit.

The Holy Spirit and God's word

Secondly, we need to remember that the Holy Spirit always operates in line with the word of God—for he himself has written that word, and he does not change. We see this truth in the very first paragraph of Scripture. When darkness covered the earth, *the Spirit of God* brooded upon it, and *the Word of God* went forth—'Let there be light.' And the joint operation of that creative word and of the Holy Spirit brought light where there was formerly darkness; it brought fullness and form where previously there were emptiness and shapelessness (Gen 1:1-3).

The new birth is attributed to the implantation of the

word of God in us (1 Pet 1:23), as well as to the operation of the Holy Spirit (Titus 3:5). Sanctification likewise is the result of the working of God's word and of the Holy Spirit in our lives (Jn 17:17; 2 Thess 2:13). In the same manner, the fullness of the Holy Spirit and being filled with the word of God go together. This becomes clear when we compare Ephesians 5:18-6:9 with Colossians 3:15-22. In the Ephesian passage we are told that giving thanks, praising God and submitting to one another in Christ-like home relationships, is the result of being filled with the Spirit. Whereas in the Colossian passage, these same things are said to be the result of being filled with the word of God.

We need to recognize this truth if we are to be balanced Christians. A steam-engine needs not only steam in order to move forward, but also rail-tracks. We need the steam of God's Spirit if we are to make spiritual progress, but we also need the rails of God's word to keep us from going astray. One is not more important than the other. Both are equally important. Some who claim to be full of steam have ignored the rails and got stuck in the mud. Placing a premium on experience, they have not been careful to test everything by God's word, and as a result have gone off the track. Like a derailed engine blowing its whistle furiously, many of them make a lot of noise in their meetings, but there is no spiritual progress—no growth in Christ-likeness—in their lives.

Some others have gone to the opposite extreme. Although they have kept on the rails, they have despised the need for fullness of steam in the engine (or have imagined that they have the fullness when they haven't), and they are stuck too. They emphasize the importance of the word of God and are careful about every jot and tittle in it—they keep admiring and polishing the rails. But they don't recognize that they need to be filled with the Holy Spirit. They are fundamental in their doctrines, all right—the rails are perfectly straight—but there is not sufficient steam to move the engine. They are dead right in their doctrines, but they are also both *dead* and right!

Let us avoid both extremes.

Our limited knowledge

Thirdly, we must recognize that even the best among us do not know *everything* about the Holy Spirit and his workings. Some Christians give the impression that they have all the answers concerning everything that relates to the Holy Spirit. They have analysed the biblical teaching on the subject and neatly pigeon-holed every verse. I'm terribly wary of such people, for I know they are wrong. We do *not* know everything. We know only in part—and especially when it concerns the ministry of the Spirit. We need to acknowledge that our finite, sinful minds are not able to apprehend fully the greatness and the vastness of God the Holy Spirit.

A. W. Tozer has said that the most profound statement in the Bible is found in Ezekiel 37:3, where Ezekiel says, 'O Lord God, thou knowest.' We know to a certain extent. But we all come to a point where we have to say, 'Lord God, I know this much, but there is so much beyond this that I don't know. I have just come to the fringe of Truth.' As Job said, 'These are but the outskirts of his ways. And how small a whisper do we hear of him! But the thunder of his power who can understand?' (Job 26:14, American Standard Version). Such an attitude will save us from a lot of carnal dogmatism on matters concerning the Holy Spirit, on which the Bible does not give us clear instruction. It will also give us a greater tolerance of others who do not see eye-to-eye with us on the Spirit's ministry. They may be wrong, but so may we. That which is clearly revealed in Scripture is for our instruction, but beyond that we are not to speculate (Deut 29:29).

No short-cuts

Fourthly, let us remember that there is no short-cut to the Spirit-filled life—no easy formula that guarantees success. In our day when push-buttons have replaced hard manual labour, and when man has generally accepted a philosophy of easy, comfortable living, Christians can all unconsciously bring this attitude into spiritual matters as well. The result is that we can think that there must be some simple formula for being filled with the Holy Spirit: take steps one, two and three—and lo and behold, we are filled! But we don't find any such formula in the Bible. We must beware of trying to reduce the Holy Spirit's operation in a person's life into a set of formulas. The fullness of the Spirit is not a mechanical matter but a matter of life—and spiritual life cannot be expressed in formulas.

Don't boast that you are filled

Fifthly, a fact to be noticed is that in the New Testament, although we read of certain people being referred to as 'full of the Spirit' (Acts 6:5; 11:24), no one ever testified to being full of the Spirit himself.

I am *not* now referring to the baptism in the Spirit (or 'receiving the Spirit',) as it is called in some passages), which is the initial experience of being filled with the Spirit. Concerning this, the apostles expected every believer to have a clear testimony as to whether he had received the Spirit or not (Acts 19:2; Gal 3:2). But in Ephesians 5:18, Paul exhorted the Ephesian Christians (who had already been baptized in the Spirit) to be continuously filled with the Spirit (literal translation). Those who walk in the Spirit in this continuous fullness could be referred to as men and women full of the Spirit. But this is something for others to notice, not for us to testify to. When Moses' face shone with the glory of God, others saw it, but he himself was ignorant of it.

To be full of the Spirit is to be full of the Spirit of Christ; and it is by the fruit of Christ-likeness in our character that others will know that we are Spirit-filled. There is no need for us to testify concerning this, for our life will speak louder than our words.

Paul's example

There is perhaps no clearer description of the Spirit-filled life than in Paul's statement in Galatians 2:20, 'I have been crucified with Christ; it is no longer I who live, but Christ who lives in me.' For what is the purpose of the fullness of the Spirit if not to reproduce the life of Jesus in us? And so the measure in which our self-life is crucified and the Christ-life manifested in us, is the true measure of our experience of the fullness of the Holy Spirit.

Paul told the Galatian Christians, 'Brethren, I beseech you, become as *I am*' (Gal 4:12). He was one who could ask others to follow his example. He did *not* have to say, 'Don't look at me, but look at Christ.' He repeatedly urged others to look at the example of his own life and to follow him as he followed Christ (1 Cor 4:16; Phil 3:17). He had such a satisfying Christian experience that even when in chains, he could tell King Agrippa that in spite of all that Agrippa possessed in the world, he only wished that Agrippa could 'become as *I am* [spiritually]' (Acts 26:29). He was not boasting, for he said elsewhere, '*By the grace of God* I am what *I am*' (1 Cor 15:10).

Let us then look at the life and ministry of the apostle Paul to see some of the characteristics of the Christ-life.

We shall consider eight passages from Scripture where Paul describes his life and service, using this very same phrase, '*I am.*'

We shall look first at the characteristics of Spirit-filled service and then at the characteristics of the Spirit-filled life.

SPIRIT-FILLED SERVICE

There are four things that I would like to mention concerning Spirit-filled service, from the words of the apostle Paul.

A love-slave of God

First of all, Spirit-filled service is *the service of a love-slave.* In Acts 27:23 Paul refers to 'the God to whom I belong and whom I worship'. He was a love-slave of his God. He retained no right to his own life. He had given everything to his Master.

The only proper basis for our consecration is a recognition of the fact that we belong wholly to God in the first place. Giving ourselves to God out of gratitude for what he has done for us, though good in itself, is not the true basis for Christian consecration. Love for Christ can be the impelling *motive* in our service for the Lord. But the *basis* on which we should dedicate our lives to God is the fact that he has purchased us on the cross. We are therefore now God's own property, and have no right to ourselves.

And so, when a person gives his entire life to God, he is not doing God a great favour. No! He is only returning to God what he had stolen from him. If I were to steal a man's money and later, convicted of my sin, were to return it to him, I would certainly not be doing that man a favour. I would go to him as a repentant thief. And that is the only proper attitude in which we can approach God when we go to give our lives to him. God has purchased us. When we recognize that, we arrive at the only proper basis for consecration.

Paul was a love-slave of the Lord. Like the Hebrew slave, who could go free in the seventh year of his service but chose to continue in that service because he loved his master (Ex 21:1-6), Paul served his Lord. He was not a hired servant who worked for wages, but one who served without any rights of his own. The service of a love-slave is beautifully summed up in the following poem:

I'm but a slave!
I have no freedom of my own,
I cannot choose the smallest thing,
Nor e'en my way.
I'm a slave!
Kept to do the bidding of my Master;
He can call me night or day.
Were I a servant, I could claim wages—
Freedom, sometimes anyway.
But I was *bought*!
Blood was the price my Master paid for me,
And I am now his slave—
And evermore will be.
He takes me here, he takes me there,
He tells me what to do;
I just obey, that's all—
I trust him too.

This is what it means to be a love-slave. God is looking for those who are so yielded to him that they are always looking to him to show them what *he* wants them to do, and not busy doing what *they* feel they should do for God. A slave does not go around doing whatever he feels like. No. The slave asks, 'Master, what do *you* want me to do?' And he does what he is told. The Bible says, 'The most important thing about a servant is that he does just what his master tells him to' (1 Cor 4:2, TLB).

The Lord says,

I'm seeking for one who will wait and watch
For my beckoning hand, my eye;
Who will work in my manner, the work I give,
And the work I give not, pass by.
And oh the joy that is brought to me
When one such as this I can find,
A man who will do all my will—who is set
To study his Master's mind.

'I sought for a man,' the Lord once said, 'but I found none' (Ezek 22:30). He is looking for love-slaves today. But he finds so few.

Serving others

Secondly, Spirit-filled service is *a service that recognizes its debt to others.* Paul said, '*I am* under obligation both to Greeks [civilized] and to barbarians [uncivilized]' (Rom 1:14). God has given us a treasure to share with the world. We are like postmen who go on their rounds with bags full of money and money-orders to be given to various people. Such a postman remains in debt to those people until he has finished paying off to each one their due. He may have thousands of pounds in his bag, but not one penny of it is his. He is a debtor.

The apostle Paul recognized a similar debt when God entrusted him with the message of the gospel. He knew it had to be given out. And he also knew that he would remain in debt to others until he had given them the message of salvation. After twenty-five years spent in preaching the good news, Paul still says, 'I am a debtor,' and he tells the Roman Christians that he is now ready to come to Rome to clear his debt to the people of Rome. Notice the three 'I am's of Paul in Romans 1:14-16; '*I am* under obligation . . . *I am* eager . . . *I am* not ashamed of the gospel.'

Spirit-filled service is outgoing. Recognizing its debt to others, it is always ready to go and discharge that debt. The evidence of the Spirit's fullness and the beauty of the Christ-life are seen not in thrilling emotional experiences but in a passion in the heart which says:

> I am Thy slave, Thy bondslave; nevermore
> Will I be free from this fierce urge within,
> To spread from race to race, and shore to shore
> The joyful news of freedom from all sin.
>
> Give me the souls of men, or else I die,
> Give me the love that does not count the cost,
> Give me the faith all barriers to defy,
> Give me the joy of bringing home the lost.

Yes. Spirit-filled service is perpetually outgoing. It is concerned with the needs of others and does not just consider its own satisfaction. Christ himself never sought his own satisfaction (Rom 15:3).

It needs to be emphasized in our day that the Spirit's fullness and his gifts are not given merely for our emotional satisfaction. Much less are they given for exhibition to others. 'Exhibitionism is common to the kindergarten,' says Tozer. God wants us to be spiritually mature, and when we are, our passion will be neither emotionalism nor exhibitionism, but evangelism and building the church.

E. L. Cattell, in his excellent book *The Spirit of Holiness,* says that there are five perils in emotionalism of which we need to beware. I have found these very helpful myself, and list them below:

(1) The peril of losing sincerity in emotional form—feeling that God is not present in a meeting until that meeting has been worked up to a certain emotional pitch and a certain noise level! We recognize God's presence by faith and not by feelings, for God dwells not in our emotions but in our spirits.

(2) The danger of seeking emotional excitement instead of God himself. Ecstasy becomes the god of some Christians.

(3) The peril of adverse witness when emotional expression is not kept under control. We shouldn't nauseate others by parading our piety before them. God is a God of order and he never calls us to go against principles of decency and order in our meetings. And we shouldn't call other people unspiritual just because they don't accept our crudities. Grace accepts torture, but it never tortures others.

(4) The danger of wasting our energies. It is extremely harmful to work up our emotions with thrilling experiences, if we don't simultaneously give expression to them by going out to meet the spiritual and physical needs of others.

(5) The peril of false holiness. Satan can sidetrack us through emotional thrills. If you have offended your wife or some other person, God will want you to apologize to her/him before fellowship with God can be restored in your life. But you can have such a nice *feeling* in a high-pitched emotional meeting or in a time of prayer in tongues, that you can be deceived into believing that you are pleasing God—when you obviously cannot be, for the main issue has not yet been settled. It may be more spectacular and less humiliating for you to speak in tongues than to go and ask for forgiveness from that wounded individual. But God expects you to do the latter first. Otherwise you deceive yourself with an illusive holiness.

I am not devaluing our emotions. God has created us with them and he does not want us to be like stones. But let us not forget that Spirit-filled service is always outgoing, thinking of its debt to others, and not just satisfying itself with experiences in the emotional realm.

We must also remember two important facts:

(a) Any experience received in an emotionally tense meeting may have been merely self-induced, and not from God at all.

(b) Any experience that makes a person lose control of himself is certainly not from God.

God does not want us to live depending on our feelings. He wants us to live by faith. This is why God sometimes allows us to *feel* spiritually dry. Such feelings of dryness are not always an indication of sin in our lives. They are often God's attempts to shake us out of our dependence on feelings.

We need to walk carefully in these days, for the Devil is leading many astray through an over-emphasis on emotions. If we want to be delivered from Satan's snares, let us remember that the beauty of the Christ-life is seen in an outgoing life.

Human insufficiency

Thirdly, Spirit-filled service is *a service that is conscious of human insufficiency*. Notice Paul's words in 2 Corinthians 10:1—'*I am* base among you' (AV)—or, in other words, 'I don't have an impressive personality.' Tradition tells us that the apostle Paul was only 4 feet 10 inches tall. He was bald, and beset by an eye-disease. He did not have a filmstar-like personality. The success of his labours did not depend on any human factor, for there was nothing attractive about his appearance or his speech.

Concerning his preaching, Paul writes to the

Corinthians, 'I was with you in weakness and in much fear and trembling' (1 Cor 2:3). When he preached, he felt conscious of his weakness, rather than of the power of God flowing through him. This is Spirit-filled service—for remember that a church was established in heathen Corinth as a result of Paul's preaching.

When the Spirit of God speaks through a man, the man himself is not usually conscious of being God's mouthpiece. I'm always wary of those folk who are so sure, when they stand in the pulpit, that God is speaking through them (and who are not hesitant to say so). My experience with such people has often been that God has never spoken through them at all. They've just had conceited ideas of being prophetic voices. The man through whom God speaks is very often not conscious of that fact at all. The apostle Paul says in one of his writings, '*I think* I am giving you counsel from God's Spirit when I say this ' (1 Cor 7:40, TLB). He was not *sure* whether God was speaking through him. Yet we know that it was God's voice, for what Paul wrote has been included in Scripture. But Paul himself was unaware of it.

Yes, Spirit-filled service is one that is conscious of human insufficiency. As Paul says, 'When I am weak, then I am strong' (2 Cor 12:10). The Spirit-filled servant of God goes again and again to God, like the man in the parable, saying, 'I have nothing to give others. Please give me the living bread' (Lk 11:5-8). The Lord's servant is perpetually conscious of his own insufficiency.

Let us not have any mistaken ideas of Spirit-filled service. It has no great awareness of God's power but on the contrary of weakness. God's power is manifested effectively through those who recognize their weakness.

Fulfilling our calling

Fourthly, Spirit-filled service is *a service that fulfils*

God's specific calling. In Colossians 1:23, 25 (AV) Paul says, '*I am* made a minister'; and in 1 Timothy 2:7 (AV), '*I am* ordained . . . an apostle'—ordained by the nail-pierced hands of Jesus, and not by any earthly ritual. God called Paul to be an apostle. This calling was *given* to him, as he himself says in Colossians 1:25. It was God's gift—not something that he had achieved. He also says in the same verse that this calling was given him for others. It was a stewardship entrusted to him by God for the work of building up the church.

God has a specific calling for each of us. It is futile to ask God to make us into something that he has not called us to be—for the Holy Spirit decides what gift each of us should have. Paul was called to be an apostle. But not everyone has such a calling. What we *do* need to seek God's face about is for power to do that to which he *has* called us. 'See that you fulfil the ministry which *you* have received in the Lord,' was Paul's advice to Archippus (Col 4:17).

God does not put square pegs into round holes. He knows what his church needs at a particular time in a particular place, and he prepares each of us (if we are submissive) for a specific task—which may be quite different from what we ourselves want to do. 'Is everyone an apostle? Of course not. Is everyone a preacher or prophet? No. Are all teachers? Does everyone have the power to do miracles? Can everyone heal the sick? Of course not. Does God give all of us the ability to speak in languages we've never learned [tongues]? . . . No' (1 Cor 12:29-30, TLB). But God has placed each of these gifts in the body of Christ. The important thing for us is to recognize what our gift and calling are and to exercise that gift and fulfil that calling. Spirit-filled service is service that fulfils that specific calling which God gives us.

If there is one gift that the New Testament specifically

encourages us to seek, it is the gift of prophecy (1 Cor 14:39). This is perhaps the most needed gift in the church today. A prophetic ministry is one that rebukes, corrects, challenges, enlightens, encourages and builds up (1 Cor 14:3). We need to pray that God will give us prophets in our churches, who will speak the truth of God, without fear or favour—men of a different calibre from professional religious scribes who are more interested in salary, status and popularity.

May the Lord help us each one to seek his face earnestly to find out what his calling is.

THE SPIRIT-FILLED LIFE

Let us look at four characteristics of the Spirit-filled life—again from the life of the apostle Paul.

Perfect contentment

The Spirit-filled life is, first of all, *a life of perfect contentment*. In Philippians 4:11 Paul says, 'In whatever state I am, *I am* content.' And such contentment brings with it fullness of joy and peace. Hence Paul speaks of joy and peace in verses 4 and 7 of the same chapter.

We can praise God only when we are perfectly content with all his dealings with us. If we believe in a God who is sovereign and who can therefore make everything that befalls us work together for our good, then we can be truly content in all circumstances. Then we can praise the Lord, like Habakkuk, even when the trees in our garden don't bear fruit, when our flock dies and when we have suffered heavy financial loss—or in any situation. Ephesians 5:18-20 indicates that the result of the infilling of the Holy Spirit is an outflow of praise to God.

The apostle Paul could rejoice even when he was

locked up in prison, with his feet in the stocks (Acts 16:24-25). He was content even there and found nothing to complain about. This is one of the first marks of the Spirit-filled life. When murmuring is found in a Christian, it is an indication that he, like the Israelites who murmured against God in the wilderness, has still not entered the promised land of victory.

Growth in holiness

Secondly, the Spirit-filled life is *a life of growth in holiness.* As a man's own life increases in holiness so does his consciousness of the absolute holiness of God. The two go together. In fact, the latter is one of the tests of whether a person really has the former.

Paul said '*I am* the least of the apostles' (1 Cor 15:9); '*I am* the very least of all the saints' (Eph 3:8); '*I am* the foremost of sinners' (1 Tim 1:15). Paul enjoyed a life of victory over sin, yet the closer he walked with God, the more he was conscious of the corruption in his flesh. He recognized that no good thing could be found in his flesh (Rom 7:18). Charles Simeon once said that the principal mark of regeneration is a detesting of oneself. This is taught in Scripture too. In Ezekiel 36:26-27, 31, God says, 'A new heart I will give you, and a new spirit I will put within you. . . . And I will put my Spirit within you. . . . Then you will loathe yourselves for your iniquities.' Only such a man will be able to fulfil the command in Philippians 2:3 to esteem others as better than himself. Having seen the corruption of his flesh, he will no longer despise anyone else.

The Spirit-filled man does not merely seek to give others the impression that he is growing in holiness, but will actually be doing so. He will not merely testify of experiences, but will have such holiness in his life that others will be drawn to him, to know the secret of his life.

True holiness comes only to the man who seeks after it with all his heart, and not to the one who has merely the correct teaching in his head. The secret of holiness is discovered not (as some think) through a study of Greek words and tenses in the New Testament, but through a wholehearted and sincere desire to please God. God looks at our hearts, not at our brains! And if we have understood the doctrine correctly, the proof of it will be in the life of Jesus being manifested in us.

A crucified life

Thirdly, the Spirit-filled life is *a life that is crucified.* Paul said, '*I am* crucified with Christ' (Gal 2:20, AV). We have already seen something of the meaning of the cross in the last two chapters. We have seen that the way of the cross is the way that leads to the fullness of the Spirit. But every time the cross leads to the Spirit, the Spirit leads back to the cross. The Spirit and the cross are inseparable.

The cross is a symbol of weakness, shame and death. The apostle Paul had perplexities, sorrows and tears in his life (see 2 Cor 1:8; 4:8; 6:10; 7:5). He was considered a fool and a fanatic. He was often treated like refuse by others (1 Cor 4:13). All this is not incongruous with the Spirit's fullness. On the contrary, the Spirit-filled man will find God leading him further and further down the pathway of humiliation and death-to-himself.

The Spirit-filled man is one who does not care for the honour of men. He accepts humiliation and reproach gladly. He glories in nothing but the cross (Gal 6:14). He does not glory in his gifts and abilities, nor even in his deeper life experiences. He glories only in dying to himself perpetually.

The cross is also the symbol of divine love. God's love for man was manifested in Christ dying on a cross for men. Such love characterizes the Spirit-filled man as well. Between him and every other person there is a cross on which he dies to himself in order to love the other. This is the real meaning of love.

Watchman Nee, in his booklet *Two Principles of Conduct,* tells the story of two Christian farmers in China who had their fields halfway up a mountain slope and who would get up early in the morning and water their fields during the day. Some other farmers, who had their fields lower down, came one night and dug a hole in their irrigation channels and let all the water flow down from the upper fields to the lower ones. This happened for seven days in succession and the two Christians wondered what to do. They finally decided that as believers they should show these other farmers the love of Christ. And so they got up the next morning and watered the lower fields first, and then their own. They put a cross between them and the other farmers and died to their own rights on it. Those non-Christian farmers, when they saw this being done for two or three days, were broken, and came to the Christians and said, 'If this is Christianity, we want to know more about it.'

Jesus said that when the Holy Spirit came upon his disciples, they would receive power to be his witnesses. The word 'witness', in the original Greek, is a word from which we get the word 'martyr'. So the literal meaning of Acts 1:8 is that when the Holy Spirit came upon the disciples, they would receive power to be martyrs—martyrs, not just in the sense of dying once on a stake, but martyrs who would die to themselves daily. And so a Spirit-filled witness is one who lives the crucified life.

Continuous enlargement

Fourthly, the Spirit-filled life is *a life that is continuously seeking greater degrees of fullness. 'I am* pressing on,' says Paul nearly thirty years after his conversion, as he was drawing to the end of his life (Phil 3:14). He still has not attained. He is seeking a still greater degree of the fullness of God in his life, and is therefore straining every spiritual muscle towards this goal. 'I am not perfect [complete],' he says in Philippians 3:12. But in verse 15 (AV) he seems to say the exact opposite: 'Let us therefore, as many as be perfect [complete], be thus minded.' This is the paradox of the Spirit-filled life—complete, and yet not complete; in other words, full and yet desiring a greater degree of fullness.

The Spirit-filled state is not a static one. There are greater and greater degrees of fullness. The Bible says that the Holy Spirit leads us from one degree of glory to another (2 Cor 3:18)—or, in other words, from one degree of fullness to another. A cup can be full of water; so can a bucket; so can a tank; and so can a river. But there is a vast difference of quantity between the fullness in the cup and the fullness in the river.

The newborn convert can be filled with the Spirit immediately on conversion. The apostle Paul was a Spirit-filled man at the end of his life. But there is a vast difference between the fullness of the newborn convert and the fullness of the mature apostle. The former is like a full cup whereas the latter is like a full river.

The Holy Spirit is constantly seeking to enlarge our capacity, so that he can fill us to a greater degree. This is where the cross comes in. There can be no enlargement in our lives if we avoid the pathway of the cross. This is why the Corinthian Christians were so shallow. They gloried in gifts and ignored the cross. And so Paul exhorts them again and again in his two epistles to them to accept the cross in their lives. He exhorts them to be thereby enlarged (2 Cor 6:13).

If we accept the cross consistently in our lives, we shall find the cup becoming a bucket, the bucket becoming a tank, the tank becoming a river and the river becoming many rivers. At each stage, as our capacity enlarges, we shall need to be filled and filled again. Thus will be fulfilled in us the promise of the Lord Jesus, 'Rivers of living water shall flow from the inmost being of anyone who believes in me. (He was speaking of the Holy Spirit . . .)' (John 7:38-39, TLB).

This also explains why Paul exhorts the Ephesian Christians to 'be continuously being filled with the Spirit' (Eph 5:18). Paul obviously never believed in a once-for-all experience that met every need. What he is speaking of here is a continuous enlargement of capacity for greater degrees of fullness.

Paul himself accepted the cross always. He says in 2 Cor 4:10 (AV), 'always bearing about in the body the dying of the Lord Jesus, that the life also of Jesus might be made manifest in our body [in ever-increasing degree].' One aspect of the cross that he accepted was the disciplining of his bodily appetites. The fullness of the Spirit is never a substitute for discipline and hard work. Paul still needed to discipline his body and bring it into subjection. He says, 'Like an athlete I punish my body, treating it roughly, training it to do what it should, *not what it wants to*' (1 Cor 9:27, TLB). He disciplined his eyes in what they read and looked at, his ears in what they listened to, and his tongue in what it spoke. He disciplined his life in every area. Thus he was enlarged.

Thank God for the crises he gives us in our lives. But let us not forget that every crisis must lead to a process. Christ is not only the Door, he is also the Way. If we enter in through the narrow gate, we have to walk the narrow way. Let us never be guilty of emphasizing the crisis to the exclusion of the process. The new birth is a crisis, but spiritual life *in the present tense* is the important thing, not just the memory of a date in the past. Some are unable to remember the date when the crisis of the new birth took place. But we don't say that a man is dead merely because he can't remember his birthday! And yet, alas, to some Christians, the testimony of an experience is the only test of life!

In relation to the fullness of the Spirit, too, the important thing is the present-tense reality of it, manifested in Christ-like living and service. The memory of an experience in the past, however wonderful, is by itself of no avail.

God is looking for men and women who will never be content with mere experiences and 'blessings', but who will take up the cross daily and follow Jesus and thus manifest in their lives and in their service the reality of those words, 'It is no longer I, but Christ that lives in me.' This, and this alone, is the Spirit-filled life.

Not I, but Christ, be honoured, loved, exalted,
Not I, but Christ, be seen, be known and heard;
Not I, but Christ, in ev'ry look and action,
Not I, but Christ, in ev'ry thought and word.

Not I, but Christ, in lowly silent labour,
Not I, but Christ, in humble earnest toil;
Christ, only Christ, no show, no ostentation;
Christ, none but Christ, the gatherer of the spoil.

Christ, only Christ, no idle word e'er falling,
Christ, only Christ, no needless bustling sound;
Christ, only Christ, no self-important bearing,
Christ, only Christ, no trace of I be found.

Not I, but Christ, my every need supplying,
Not I, but Christ, my strength and health to be;
Christ, only Christ, for spirit, soul and body,
Christ, only Christ, live then Thy life in me.

Christ, only Christ, ere long will fill my vision,
Glory excelling soon, full soon I'll see;
Christ, only Christ, my every wish fulfilling,
Christ, only Christ, my all in all to be.

Oh, to be saved from myself, dear Lord,
Oh, to be lost in Thee,
Oh, that it may be no more I,
But Christ that lives in me.

Amen and Amen.